UNDERSTANDING TECHNICAL CHANGE
AS AN EVOLUTIONARY PROCESS

PROFESSOR DR. F. DE VRIES
LECTURES IN ECONOMICS
Theory, Institutions, Policy

VOLUME 8

NORTH-HOLLAND
AMSTERDAM · NEW YORK · OXFORD · TOKYO

UNDERSTANDING TECHNICAL CHANGE AS AN EVOLUTIONARY PROCESS

RICHARD R. NELSON

Columbia University

1987

NORTH-HOLLAND
AMSTERDAM · NEW YORK · OXFORD · TOKYO

© ELSEVIER SCIENCE PUBLISHERS B.V., 1987

ISBN 0 444 70207 5

Publishers:
ELSEVIER SCIENCE PUBLISHERS B.V.
P.O. Box 1991
1000 BZ Amsterdam
The Netherlands

Sole distributors for the U.S.A. and Canada:
ELSEVIER SCIENCE PUBLISHING COMPANY, INC.
52 Vanderbilt Avenue
New York, N.Y. 10017
U.S.A.

Library of Congress Cataloging-in-Publication Data

Nelson, Richard R.
    Understanding technical change as an evolutionary process.

    (Professor Dr. F. de Vries lectures in economics ;
v. 8)
    Bibliography: p.
    1. Technological innovations--Economic aspects.
2. Technology and state.   I. Title.   II. Series.
HC79.T4N45   1987   338'.06   87-9109
ISBN 0-444-70207-5

Professor F. de Vries (1884–1958) became the first professor of economics at the Netherlands School of Economics (Rotterdam), which was founded in 1913. In 1945 he accepted an offer of the University of Amsterdam to teach economics in its Faculty of Law. On the occasion of his 70th birthday, May 2, 1954, his pupils created the Professor F. de Vries Foundation to honour a most influential teacher and a scholar of outstanding theoretical and practical wisdom.

The aim of the foundation is to regularly invite prominent economists from abroad for a series of lectures on theoretical subjects, as a stimulus to theoretical work in economics in the Netherlands.

FOREWORD

RICHARD NELSON, who is Henry R. Luce Professor of International Political Economy at Columbia University, New York, is well-known for his work on long run economic development. In a series of articles he has analysed the uncertain and irregular processes of technical change that drive dynamic competition. These studies culminated in a book he wrote together with Sidney Winter: *An Evolutionary Theory of Economic Change* (1982). Maybe the best way to summarise this work is to select two conclusions, viz. (1) to the extent that technical change is an evolutionary process, as argued in this book, it is an inherently inefficient process, (2) in contrast with simpler views of Schumpeterian competition, technical change and market structure must be understood as mutually interactive, with each affecting the other.

In the F. de Vries Lectures, held in autumn 1985, Richard Nelson discussed a questionnaire which aimed at collecting empirical information about several explaining variables of the evolutionary theory set out earlier. The results of this survey research study were given on a preliminary basis. Therefore this volume has been written after the work reached a more mature stage, so that the author was able to round off his thinking about technical development.

The empirical information has stimulated Nelson to deepen his ideas about economic change. First he repeats important parts of his evolutionary theory, but then the author goes well beyond the conclusions stated above. In doing so he investigates thoroughly the institutional reactions to the danger that free competition does not end in an efficient situation on the market. His analysis of these organisational aspects of technical advance is strongly influenced by the work of Oliver Williamson. But there remains an interesting difference. In Nelson's thinking the tendency of efficiency assumed in the evolutionary process does not eliminate diversity. On the contrary, he stresses institutional richness and tries to explain the complex and finely veined organisation of capitalist economies in the industrialised world.

The F. de Vries Foundation is very pleased to present Nelson's thought-provoking contribution. He combines in a masterly way deep theoretical insight with affinity to the functioning of organisations in economic life. This approach is fully in line with the work of the eminent economist to whose memory these lectures are dedicated.

P.H. Admiraal

CONTENTS

Chapter 1

TECHNICAL CHANGE AND ECONOMIC ANALYSIS

Technical change, and the conditions that will nurture and support a strong national performance in industries where technical change is important, are of widespread public interest these days. Over the past few years Europe has seen a rash of new government policies devised to help European industries catch and stay up with the Americans and the Japanese in high technology industries. There is much talk and writing, if not much action, in the United States about our declining technological lead. The Japanese are busy contemplating what it might mean no longer to have the United States as a clear technological leader providing targets for emulation and are trying to devise new policies for the new situation.

Economists are playing a non-trivial part in the policy debate, at least in some countries. However, our ability to contribute constructively has been limited by the fact that much of the corpus of contemporary economic analysis takes technology as a given, and exogenous. While the last decade has seen a growing body of research by economists on aspects of technical change, the field is scarcely at the center of professional attention. Also, the standard theoretical tools of modern economics were not fashioned to deal with technical change. A central argument of this essay is that if economists are to recognize technical change as important and endogenous, some far reaching changes are required in terms of how we model economic activity more generally.

(A) The renaissance of interest in technical change

The recent surge of interest by economists in the topic might usefully be regarded as a return to our intellectual origins which, somehow, had been abandoned. The great classical economists were quite aware of the industrial revolution going on around them and technical advance, at least in manufacturing, played an important role in their analysis. The first part of Adam Smith's *Wealth of Nations* is mostly about what nowadays would be called technical change and economic growth. Contained therein are fascinating discussions of the role of science in technical change and of learning by doing. Marx's analysis of the dynamics of capitalist systems has technical change, forced by competition, in a central place. In his discussion of industries subject to increasing returns, Marshall clearly had in mind technical change that occurred as an industry grew.

However, during the first half of the twentieth century the interests of economists turned away from technical change. Attention began to concentrate on long run steady state 'equilibrium' configurations, which had played an ancillary role in classical economics. Concern with the dynamics of long term change, which had been central, dropped away. From Walras on, analyses of equilibrium conventionally took technology as a given. The microeconomics of the post World War II era, which grew out of Hicks' *Value and Capital* and Samuelson's *Foundations*, starts out with given production sets or functions. Macroeconomics, during the 1930s and in the early post war period, concerned itself almost exclusively with inflation and unemployment, cyclic or chronic, with very little concern for factors influencing the pace and pattern of long run economic growth.

Since the middle 1950s, there has been a gradual, but spreading, renaissance of interest in technical change. The renewed interest has had several sources.

There was, first of all, the empirical work on long run economic change in the United States, done under the auspices of the National Bureau of Economic Research and the Committee on Economic Development, and the interpretation of the findings. Output in the United States was found to have grown at a rate significantly faster than the rate of increase of a price-weighted index of inputs.[1] The scholars participating in this endeavor, particularly Abramovitz, Denison, Fabricant, and Kendrick, carefully noted that a wide variety of factors probably lay behind this difference, but all of them stressed the advance of technology. The proposition that technical advance had been an important source of growth was given orthodox analytic foundations by Solow, in his article 'Technical Change and the Aggregate Production Function'. During the 60s and 70s, a considerable number of economists engaged themselves in growth accounting exercises, in which one of the sources of growth was technical change, and in the fitting of production functions which admitted technical advance.

[1] For a review of the literature, see Nelson (1981).

Another source of interest of technical change stemmed from Schumpeter's *Capitalism, Socialism, and Democracy*. There he argued forcefully that the microeconomic analysis which had come to dominate mainline economics was missing the point by focusing on competition in a static context. He argued that in many industries technical advance was the principal weapon of competition, and that in terms of the social benefits, competition induced innovation was vastly more important than competition induced marginal cost pricing. He further proposed that, in contrast with orthodox views about the relationship between market structure and competition, a market structure involving large firms with a reasonable amount of market power was both inevitable and desirable, where innovation was potentially important.

During the 1960s and 1970s a number of industrial organization economists took the bait Schumpeter laid down and a loud debate ensued about the relative importance of big firms, small firms, established firms and new firms, in industrial organization. There was also some solid, if inconclusive, empirical investigation of the matter and a surge of models aimed to explore the links between technical advance and market structure.[2]

A third source of renewed interest was located initially largely in agricultural economics and was concerned with the returns to publicly financed R and D viewed as an investment, and the rationale for public investments in R and D. Here Griliches' study of hybrid corn set the pattern show-

---

[2] This literature has been reviewed in several places. Perhaps the best coverage is provided by Kamien and Schwartz (1982).

ing, as did many subsequent studies, that the social rate of return on public investments in R and D in agriculture had been extremely high.[3] Other work probed at the rate of return in public R and D in the field of health. Several economists began to explore, theoretically and empirically, the reasons for and the nature of public finance of research and development. The notion that basic scientific knowledge is, or ought to be, a 'public good' became widely accepted. There were a few studies of 'spillover' from military R and D into commercial use. The market failure language, and various specific models, began to get applied to industrial R and D activity. Some models showed that private profit incentives led to an underinvestment in R and D; other models showed that market competition led to overinvestment and inefficient allocation of R and D. In any case, economists began to get into their heads that one could not automatically invoke the twin theorems of welfare economics to argue that a competitive market economy would automatically generate an optimal magnitude and allocation of R and D, and that there was room for, and examples of, fruitful public investments in R and D.

Leontief's calculations, which indicated that the United States did not in general export capital intensive goods, provided another starting place for renewed interest in technical advance.[4] His analysis set in train the development of a

[3] See Griliches (1958). A recent survey of analysis of the returns to public R and D spending is provided by Kalos (1983).

[4] The key article is Leontief 'Domestic Production and Foreign Trade: The American Capital Position Re-examined' (1966).

number of models, and a considerable amount of empirical research, organized around the idea that countries like the United States have a comparative advantage in new products, and in industries where product and process technical advance is rapid. In some cases, but not all, this analysis was linked to the notion of a 'product cycle' in which, as a product or an industry matured and technical advance slowed down, comparative advantage shifted from high income countries with considerable research and development resources, to low income countries without much in the way of a research and development system.

In the various lines of research described above, the interest in technical advance was induced by an original interest in a broader topic – economic growth, industrial organization, the efficacy of public investments, patterns of international trade. It is interesting and revealing, that these various bodies of research and writing have tended to stand separate from each other intellectually. Researchers on certain kinds of questions stress externalities; researchers on other kinds implicitly deny them. Differing assumptions are made about market structure. What unifies the various areas of research is an understanding, or a presumption, that technical change is an important factor influencing the phenomena under consideration. In a sense, contemporary economics, from a number of different starting points, seems to be coming back to the presumption with which Adam Smith started – that technical change is an integral aspect of the workings of a modern economy. However, there is no coherence in the views of what technical change is all about.

In fact over the past two decades a lot has been learned about how technical change proceeds, the character of the activities involved, the forces bearing on them and the key institutions. A portion of this knowledge has been gleaned through the efforts of economists studying the issues listed above, but most has come about as a result of research by economists and other scholars interested in understanding technical advance as a phenomenon in its own right, as well as a force influencing economic performance.

(B) Characteristics of technical change in capitalist countries

What seem to be the essential characteristics of technical change in capitalist economies?[5] Actually, this question is somewhat too broad as posed here. There are significant inter-industry differences. Thus, technical change in aviation is not quite the same as technical change in pharmaceuticals. And countries differ as well. Aviation R and D is organized quite differently in Europe than in the United States. I shall come to some of these important differences later. However, some generalizations do seem possible.

One of these, and a feature of technical change that seems to apply in socialist systems as well as capitalist ones, is that there is often considerable uncertainty about the best way to achieve any particular desired technical advance, and experts differ among themselves regarding the bets they think

[5] For a survey, pointed towards an evolutionary theory, see Nelson and Winter (1982a, particularly Chapter 11).

ought to be laid down. Thus, during the 1950s aviation experts differed as to whether the first generation of passenger jets ought to be powered by turbojet engines, or turboprop engines. After the transistor came out, computer designers differed regarding whether, and when, to try to build computers around transistors. There was similar divergence regarding the adoption of integrated circuits.

There are a wide variety of activities that can reduce these uncertainties, ranging from basic research aimed to enhance general understanding of certain key relationships, to more narrowly oriented applied research focused on trying to resolve particular problems germane to one or more of the candidate designs, to development committed to trying to bring a particular design to operational status and in the course of doing so revealing much about its strengths and weaknesses. A key characteristic of technical change in capitalist countries is that these activities usually are done in a pluralistic context, in which several different firms are involved in exploring the alternatives for themselves.

In addition, though partly as a result, a number of different departures tend to pass into actual practice. In the cases above, Lockheed and Vickers bet on turboprops, while Boeing and Douglas bet on turbojets. Each company actually developed and produced, and got into commercial operation, vehicles of the design they were betting on. Different computer manufacturers made different bets as to when to get out of vacuum tubes and into transistors, and later, into integrated circuits, and the companies that went ahead did so with different designs. At the present time, a number of pharmaceutical companies are working on new drugs that have the promise of dealing better with various forms of cancer. In many cases a new departure will not turn out, on net, to have advantages vis-à-vis established technologies. In other cases, several new departures will, but one will clearly dominate the others. In other cases, several innovations will find different niches, while others will find no profitable use given the competing technologies. Put more generally, in capitalist economies the inherent uncertainties regarding innovation are resolved in large part by actual introduction and trial use of a wide variety of alternative departures.

With the vision of hindsight this looks like a very wasteful process. There ought to be a less costly way of finding out which of a set of alternatives is best other than actually building and trying each. But, in fact, most of the clearly poor ideas are screened out through analysis and research. Development and actual production go forth only on designs that someone or some firm feels are sufficiently promising to bet on with real money. It is quite possible that if some firms had known what other firms knew, or what other firms were going to do, the former would have tried something else or thrown in the sponge. But, to someone who is not aware of the record, it is surprising how often near consensus bets proved to be busts in actual practice, and long shots came through. The capitalist innovation system, with its pluralism and actual obstacles to coordination, bears the costs but has the advantages of generating a variety of new departures, and of letting ex post selection play a major role in separating the wheat from the chaff, the winners from the losers.

This assertion immediately raises two kinds of questions. Selection: on the basis of what criteria? And through what mechanisms?

In the discussion that follows I shall limit my attention to industries where firms are in business to make a profit, simply noting that this cuts out a lot of economic activity and technical change. In this setting, a product innovation is a winner if it can be sold to customers in a quantity and at a price which more than covers total costs. A process innovation is a winner if it enables lower cost production than an available alternative process and, in addition, can be operated profitably. What innovations will be profitable and which will not, clearly depends on customer tastes and product and factor prices, as well as prevailing technology. In many industries it also depends on the nature of regulation, subsidy, protection and other variables not customarily considered in standard economic models of competition.

Aside from intra-firm substitution of one process or product for another by the innovator, there are two different kinds of mechanisms through which innovations that prove profitable replace the techniques they dominate. One is through expansion of production and growth of the company that introduces a profitable innovation. The second is through adaptive imitation by competing firms. The relative importance of these two different mechanisms differs from industry to industry, and depends on such variables as the ability of the innovating firm to hold off imitation. I shall consider some of the key variables and inter-industry differences later.

In competitive industries there are selection forces operative on firms, as well as on techniques. These are not the same thing for two reasons. First, firms other than the innovator may ultimately be able to use or produce the innovation. Second, in general, while there are exceptions, the economic viability of a firm is not tied to one particular product or process, but rather involves its mix of products and processes and the adequacy of changes in these over time.

In an industry where innovation is an important aspect of competition, the ability of a firm to survive depends on the effectiveness of its research and development laboratories, on its ability to exploit its innovations and protect them, or to quickly match anything that its competitors do. As with respect to particular techniques, in many industries there may be niches for different kinds of strategies regarding innovation and imitation. Indeed, in many industries one can observe the continuing coexistence of some firms whose strategies call for striving to be at the forefront, and other firms which are content to lay back a little behind the frontier while incurring lower research and development expenses. I shall examine a model of such an asymmetric dynamic equilibrium later in this essay.

(C) Technical change as an evolutionary process

The title of this essay is understanding technical advance as an evolutionary process. While up to now I have not used that term in my description of the essential features of technical change in capitalist economies, I now do want to use it to refer to the complex of features I have just described, and to facilitate understanding of the differences between the kinds of models that Sidney Winter and I have developed, and the more standard neo-classical models incorporating technical change. What do Winter and I mean when we say that economic change in general, and technical change in particular, should be understood as an evolutionary process?[6]

Most emphatically we do not mean blindly picking up ideas and models from biology. While we would agree with Marshall that there is much that economists can learn by looking to what the biologists do, social, economic and technical change must be understood on their own terms. Thus, by an evolutionary theory we mean to include a relatively large class of models of change, with evolutionary theory in biology being a special case, and evolutionary theory of technical change being another special case.

By an evolutionary theory, I mean one that contains the following components. First, a mechanism that introduces novelties to the system. While this mechanism may have a bias for generating certain kinds of novelties, and may be predictably responsive in a broad way to certain outside forces, in an evolutionary theory its workings also involve a significant random element. Second, some understandable mechanism that 'selects on' entities present in the system, expanding the relative importance of some and diminishing that of others. I use the term entities here to preserve analytical flexibility regarding what is being selected; several different kinds of things might be. By understandable selec-

---

[6] Nelson and Winter (1982a).

tion mechanism, I mean both that the forces that lead to expansion or decline be describable as processes, and that the factors lying behind competitive fitness be identifiable and to some extent predictable on the basis of the characteristics of the entities and the environmental setting. Put another way, the theory must do better than simply to assert that fitness is witnessed by survivability. I would add the following presumption about evolutionary systems: at any time there are feasible entities not present in the prevailing system that have a chance of being introduced by the novelty generator that are more fit than any presently in the system. But while most general evolutionary theorists would agree with me regarding my general characterization of an evolutionary system, some would not buy my 'presumption'.

In biology the entities are genotypes expressed as phenotypes, and the novelties are 'mutations', or new genotypes. While certain kinds of mutation are more likely than others, at the level of evolutionary theory there is a major random element in the mutation process. In some biological systems, but not all, sexual pairing each generation reshuffles the configuration of genotypes and thus complements mutation in generating and preserving variety. Natural selection works on 'inclusive fitness', meaning the ability of an entity characterized by a given set of genes to have surviving offspring, who in turn have surviving offspring, etcetera. Evolutionary biologists differ among themselves in the extent to which they put weight on mutation generating mechanisms, and in the speed with which they presume selection forces operate. Those that downplay or ignore mutation, and argue that selection works powerfully and rapidly, often have argued that the biological evolutionary system is an 'optimizing' system. But that proposition hinges on the presumption that the set of entities can for all practical purposes be taken as a given, and that exogenous environmental changes which effect the relative fitness of different genotypes proceed slowly relative to the speed of selection mechanisms.

There are several different kinds of 'entities' in Winter's and my theory of technical change in a capitalist system. There are 'techniques'. There are 'firms' with R and D strategies, which can change their techniques and even their R and D strategies, in a way quite unlike biological phenotypes which are stuck with their original set of genes. This distinction we would argue means that there is an important additional mechanism involved in 'cultural' evolution, of which technical evolution is a special case, that is absent in biological evolution. Our theory might be regarded as a special case of analysis of cultural evolution, where market values play an essential role and profit is the figure of merit, and where competitive pressures work to cut back unprofitable entities and augment profitable ones.

The novelties in our system are innovations, and we stress new techniques of production. However, within our theory it is perfectly possible for new kinds of firm R and D strategies or other new firm characteristics to emerge and to be tested by the market.

If we were to adopt the presumption that, in analysis of the dynamics of the system, innovation could be ignored, and assumed that selection pressures worked rapidly relative to changes in exogenous conditions, then our complicated dynamic models might be well approximated by neo-classical ones which presume equilibrium and maximization. As noted, some biologists make similar presumptions about the evolutionary system they are studying. However, it has been a characteristic of capitalist economies for more than two centuries that new techniques which dominate prior ones, and new institutions keep on emerging. And selection forces do not seem to operate so effectively and rapidly that inefficient techniques, R and D strategies and firms, can be presumed always to account for a trivial fraction of the whole. Further, the mechanisms generating profitable innovations are of interest in and of themselves, as also are the processes leading to decline or metamorphosis of unprofitable older forms. For all these reasons, we think it an analytic mistake to try to collapse an evolutionary theory of technical advance into a neo-classical one.

(D) Implications for economic modeling

In my experience, economists are likely to acknowledge the point that, if one is concerned with getting the details right, technical change must be understood as an evolutionary process, but argue that this has no particular implications for economic theorizing or modeling in general. There are several layers to this defense of orthodoxy.

First, for many, perhaps most, fields of economic inquiry the fact that technical change is going on is not particularly important. Therefore, there is no strong reason to build technical change explicitly into the analysis. Second, in any case, theories and models are abstractions, and the art of modeling is to cut out unnecessary complications. If one wants to build technical change explicitly into a model, one still can employ the concepts of profit maximization and equilibrium, recognizing, of course, that there is a lot of noise going on behind the scenes. Third, in any case, even if one needs to recognize the uncertainty and the diversity of behavior associated with technical progress, one can do this within the neo-classical paradigm. All one needs to do is to build in divergent expectations and friction, and treat profit maximization and equilibrium in subtle ways.

I would rejoin that the range of fields in economics where technical advance now is acknowledged to be an important element is extremely wide and that, therefore, the presumption ought to be that technical advance should be dealt with explicitly, except in special cases. I would respond, secondly, by stressing that the assumptions of maximization and equilibrium, at least as conventionally employed, lead not to a simplification but a gross misspecification of what technical change is all about. Technical change clearly is an evolutionary process; the innovation generator keeps on producing entities superior to those earlier in existence, and adjustment forces work slowly. And I would respond, finally, that if one wants to expand the set of models, that one understands as neo-classical, to include those admitting substantial diversity of expectations as well as performance and friction, and to define maximization and equilibrium so as to be consistent with this, then we are talking about the same kind of analytic animal. If our colleagues want to discuss including under the neo-classical umbrella the kinds of models Sidney Winter and I have devised, we would be happy to participate in such an ecumenical congress.

(E) Road map

The remainder of this essay is organized as follows. Chapter 2 is concerned with formal evolutionary models. I describe the general modeling art form that Winter and I have developed, and then present and analyze a number of different special models. Throughout, my concern will be to highlight the differences, as well as the similarities, between evolutionary models and neo-classical ones. Or, rather, the emphasis is on what is seen about phenomena, when they are examined through the lens of evolutionary theory, that is missed or distorted when the perspective is a neo-classical one.

In Chapter 3 I turn to characterizing inter-industry differences. My focus is on the variables that drive the evolutionary models discussed in Chapter 2. The empirical basis of the analysis is provided by a data set that my colleagues and I collected through the use of a survey research questionnaire. I describe that questionnaire and summarize some of the interesting data that can be drawn from it.

In Chapter 4 I turn to the institutions supporting technical change in industry. While most models of technical change, including those that Winter and I have developed thus far, present a very simple institutional structure, in fact in many industries the structure is quite complex, involving universities as well as for-profit business firms, public monies as well as private and modes of inter-firm cooperation, as well as competition. I review and analyze these institutional arrangements and their inter-industry differences, using data drawn from the survey research questionnaire and from other sources.

Chapter 5 is concerned with the roles played by government. I identify several different types of government R and D support programs, and describe several examples of each, basing my analysis on European and Japanese experience, as well as American. My concluding chapter summarizes the argument and pulls it together.

Chapter 2

EVOLUTIONARY MODELING

(A) Appreciative and formal theorizing

Winter and I have suggested that economic theorizing tends to proceed in two quite different styles, which we call appreciative and formal. Appreciative theorizing involves the way economists write and talk about phenomena where the emphasis is on understanding these, rather than advancing a specifically theoretical point. That way of talking and writing, however, generally involves strong theoretical presumptions about what variables are important, how they are connected, the basic processes going on, etcetera, as well as informed attention to the phenomena in question. The discussion toward the close of the preceding chapter was appreciative in style. Formal theorizing is more self-consciously analytical, more concerned with how a logical structure works, and less shaped by detailed knowledge about particular phenomena, even when it is acknowledged that part of the purpose of theory is to address these.

We have argued that when the intellectual enterprise is going well, appreciative theory and formal theory are consistent with others and their advances are superadditive. Enhanced understanding of phenomena provides challenges to formal theory to encompass the understanding in stylized form. New formal theory provides new angles from which to look at phenomena. Economists have long been attracted to evolutionary theory at an appreciative level. However, until recently there has been little work concerned with developing formal evolutionary models. Virtually all of the formal analytic work was neo-classical. Thus, the advance of an evolutionary appreciative theory was lent no support by advances in formal modeling.

In this chapter I sketch several formal analyses guided by appreciative evolutionary theory. The purpose is to explore the ways in which evolutionary models differ from neo-classical ones, and in particular to identify what they highlight that neo-classical models repress. The particular models differ from each other in important ways, connected with their difference in purpose or aim. So, too, collections of neo-classical models differ. But as with neo-classical modeling, evolutionary modeling, as we have attempted to develop the art form, is marked by several basic analytic premises and a general modeling style.

The premises have been discussed in the opening chapter. Technical innovation, and innovation more generally, is a central aspect of economic activity and ought to be modeled in terms of exploration of a choice set that is not fully known, and regarding which different actors have different beliefs. As a result of innovation by themselves or by other firms, or changes in market conditions coming from other sources, firms often find themselves in an environment that contains some surprises that will force some to adapt, or die. Ways to successfully adapt may not be obvious. These presumptions rule out notions that firm behavior is 'maximizing', and the industry as a whole is in 'equilibrium', unless one wants to be very liberal regarding the meaning of those terms. But how, then, do we model the behavior of firms?

In our evolutionary models, as in neo-classical ones, the actors are viewed as purposive and intelligent, and as operating according to a set of decision rules. As an orthodox theory, these are the best the actors know about at any time, and (metaphorically at least) some thought has been given to the matter. However, in our evolutionary theory we stress another aspect of decision rules. They are carried out as a matter of 'routine'.

In our perspective, a firm at any time is characterized largely in terms of the routines it has. At any time the firm simply *has* a set of routines, and if the analysis is pointed forward in time this is all the analyst need know. From another perspective, prevailing routines can be understood as having arisen in the firm through a series of past actions which can be interpreted as 'searches' to find better ways of doing things. However, no search is exhaustive, and in finite time only a fraction of the set of possible routines can be examined.

Firms that have better routines – production techniques, procedures for choosing alternative mixes of inputs and outputs, pricing rules, investment project screening rules, mechanisms for allocating the attention of management and the operations research staff, R and D policies – will tend to prosper and grow relative to those firms whose capabilities and behavior are less well suited to the current situation. But there are limits (as in orthodox theory, when friction or adjustment costs are admitted) to the rate at which a firm can expand or contract.

Winter and I find it valuable analytically to distinguish among three different kinds of 'routines'. First, there are those that might be called 'standard operating procedures'. In the standard theory of the firm these would be those that in the short run (fixed capital stock) determine inputs and outputs. In our various models we focus on the techniques commanded by a firm at any time, and its rules for using these in different mixes and levels. Second, there are routines that determine the investment behavior of the firm, the equations that govern its growth or decline (measured in terms of its capital stock). Third, the deliberative processes of the firm, its 'search' behavior, also are viewed as guided by routines. In principle, within our model search behavior could be focused on any one of the firms prevailing routines – its techniques, its input and output determination rules, its investment rule, or even its R and D policy. In practice, in all of the models we have built, search was assumed to uncover new production techniques. We have taken the other 'routines' as constants.

The firm, or rather the collection of firms in the industry, perhaps involving new firms coming into the industry and old firms exiting, is viewed as operating within an exogenously determined environment modeled in terms of the demand curve for the product of the industry and the supply curves of inputs purchased by firms in the industry. In all of our modeling to date we have taken these two kinds of markets as being in period by period equilibrium.

The logic of the model defines a dynamic stochastic system. We often have modeled it as a complex Markov process. A standard iteration can be described as follows. At the existing moment of time all firms can be characterized by their capital stocks and prevailing routines. Decision rules keyed to market conditions look to those conditions 'last period'. Inputs employed and outputs produced by all firms then are determined. So then are input and output prices for this period. Given the technology and other routines used by each firm, each firm's profitability is determined as well. The investment rule then determines how much each firm expands or contracts. Search routines focus on one or another aspect of the firm's behavior and capabilities, and (stochastically) come up with proposed modifications which the firm may, or may not, adopt. The system is now ready for next period's interaction.

The system may or may not have a steady state. There may or may not be a kind of dynamic equilibrium configuration. But our models are perfectly usable even if there are no equilibria, static or dynamic. They define equations of motion.

In the remainder of this chapter I shall explore four different models.[1] The first model deals with matters at the heartland of traditional economic analysis: how to analyze the substitution responses set in train by a factor price shock. The second model is concerned with analysis of productivity growth fueled by technical change. The third is of the competitive struggle among firms in industries where innovation is important. My final example is concerned with dynamic selection equilibria in which firms of different types coexist.

---

[1] Some of the following discussion follows Nelson (1986a).

(B) Firm and industry response to a factor price shock

The first topic I will explore is analysis of firm and industry response to a factor price shock, like the oil price jump of the early 1970s. This is the kind of question where it might appear, at first thought, that neo-classical theory is quite adequate, and that introducing technical change and modeling in the spirit of evolutionary theory would simply complicate or even obfuscate matters. I disagree. In this section I do not present a particular behavioral model, but rather a way of analyzing different kinds of effects of a price shock in a way that highlights the difference between neo-classical and evolutionary theory. Specific models, of course, can and have been developed.[2]

Within evolutionary theory, as within orthodox theory, a firm can be viewed at any time as having decision rules that determine its inputs and outputs, as a function of market conditions. For simplicity assume that all techniques have the same capital output ratio, and define units so that the ratio is unity. On the other hand, variable input proportions are flexible and differ across techniques. Assume that at time t firm i's decision rule governing a particular variable input, say energy, has the following general form:

$$\left(\frac{x_i}{k_i}\right) = D(P, d_i). \tag{1}$$

[2] The model discussed below was originally published in Nelson and Winter (1975). A slightly revised version is presented in Chapter 7 of Nelson and Winter (1982a).

Here the left-hand side variable is the amount of the variable input per unit of capital (or output) employed by firm i, P is the vector of output and variable input prices, and d_i is a vector of decision rule parameters, that determine $(x/k)_i$, given P. (For notational convenience I treat all differences among alternative possible decision rules, among firms and over time, as parameter differences.)

Let $X = \Sigma x_i$ and let $K = \Sigma k_i$ (all summations here are over the index i). Then, for the industry,

$$\left(\frac{X}{K}\right) = \Sigma D(P, d_i)\left(\frac{k_i}{K}\right). \tag{2}$$

The left-hand side variable is obviously total industry variable input (energy) per unit of industry capital (or output).

Even if market conditions are constant, X/K may evolve over time. The traditional comparative statics approach of price theory represses what happens to X/K over time for a given set of market conditions and focuses on the variation associated with a change in market conditions. In what follows, I will be explicit about *both* kinds of differences.

Consider two different market regimes. In regime zero, prices are at P_0 forever. Under regime one, prices are P_0 until time t and P_1 after that time.

Consider some time T greater than t. Then, under regime zero one can 'explain' X/K at time T, which may be different than it was at t, as follows:

$$\left(\frac{X}{K}\right)_0^T = \Sigma D(P_0, d_i^t)\left(\frac{k_i}{K}\right)^t$$

$$+ \Sigma[D(P_0, d_{i0}^T) - D(P_0, d_i^t)]\left(\frac{k_i}{K}\right)^t$$

$$+ \Sigma D(P_0, d_{i0}^T)\left[\left(\frac{k_i}{K}\right)_0^T - \left(\frac{k_i}{K}\right)^t\right]. \quad (3)$$

The superscripts T and t identify the time at which the variables are measured. The subscript zero has been used to tag variables that may be different at time T under regime zero than under regime one. Given this notation the first term is of course $(X/K)^t$. The second term accounts for the effects of the evolution of rules between t and T, weighted by capital stocks initially (at time t). The final term accounts for selection effects that change share weights on the final rules. And one can devise an equation, similar to (3), to show what (X/K) will be at time T, under regime one.

$$\left(\frac{X}{K}\right)_1^T = \Sigma D(P_1, d_i^t)\left(\frac{k_i}{K}\right)^t$$

$$+ \Sigma[D(P_1, d_{i1}^T) - D(P_1, d_i^t)]\left(\frac{k_i}{K}\right)^t$$

$$+ \Sigma D(P_1, d_{i1}^T)\left[\left(\frac{k_i}{K}\right)_1^T - \left(\frac{k_i}{K}\right)^t\right]. \quad (4)$$

By subtracting eq. (3) from eq. (4) one can 'account for' the *difference* in X/K at time T under the two market regimes.

$$\left(\frac{X}{K}\right)_1^T - \left(\frac{X}{K}\right)_0^T = \Sigma\,[D(P_1, d_i^t) - D(P_0, d_i^t)]\left(\frac{k_i}{K}\right)^t$$

$$+ \Sigma[D(P_1, d_{i1}^T) - D(P_1, d_i^t) - D(P_0, d_{i0}^T)$$

$$+ D(P_0, d_i^t)]\left(\frac{k_i}{K}\right)^t$$

$$+ \Sigma\left[D(P_1, d_{i1}^T)\left[\left(\frac{k_i}{K}\right)_1^T - \left(\frac{k_i}{K}\right)^t\right]\right.$$

$$\left. - D(P_0, d_{i0}^T)\left[\left(\frac{k_i}{K}\right)_0^T - \left(\frac{k_i}{K}\right)^t\right]\right]. (5)$$

Eq. (5) provides a way of analyzing the canonical question of comparative statics; what is the effect of a change in prices. The first term (or, properly, the terms under the first summation) can be viewed as the result of firms moving along the decision rules at time t in response to a change in price from P_0 to P_1. The second term reflects the fact that decision rules may evolve differently under the two regimes. The final term accounts for the difference in selection effects.

The above decomposition of the differences made by a price change could be regarded as merely a matter of accounting, without causal significance. Winter and I argue, however, that the separation is useful analytically because the three terms correspond to the operation of analytically distinguishable mechanisms.

In any case, the prototypical question of positive economic theory is: what is the sign of the difference analyzed in (5)? In particular, the focus is often on the sign of the response of intensity of use of an input to a rise in its own price. In reference to tradition, and the weight of empirical evidence, we shall call conclusions regarding this that accord with orthodox qualitative predictions 'standard' and conclusions that fail to accord 'perverse'.

Orthodox theory derives its 'standard' results from the assumption of profit maximization over a given choice set. In terms of the accounting framework above, orthodox theory may be interpreted as a theory about responses governed by decision rules. The second and third terms are not considered. My analysis with Winter stresses the importance of the second and third terms, which orthodox theory ignores.

In order to argue, within evolutionary theory, that overall industry response will be standard, it would be sufficient to show that each of the three terms in our accounting carries the sign of the standard response, or at least that their expectations do. But this can be plausibly argued.

Winter and I have no quarrel with the orthodox presumptions about the sign of the first term. Indeed we would argue that the assumptions of orthodox theory that give that sign can be considerably relaxed. One does not have to accept the view that a firm's sole objective is profit and that its built-in decision rules are 'optimal' to be comfortable with the presumption that firms do pay attention to profitability and have given some thought to whether their policies serve that objective. If firms have any routines at all for shifting among inputs in response to changes in input prices, one would expect the sign of that 'along-the-rule' effect to be standard.

But what about the second and third parts of the story? Orthodox theory ignores these, but in our view they are likely to be important. Can they lead to perverse effects? Our position is that they can, but they are unlikely to.

If innovation is affected by the changes in factor prices, it ought to be nudged in a standard direction. Even if prices did not affect the kinds of R and D activities undertaken, but firms screen their completed R and D endeavors to see if the new technologies would save on total costs, a jump in oil prices would have standard effects on innovation. Actually, one would expect significant changes in the price of an input to focus effort specifically on doing something to conserve on that particular input, or substitute away from it.

The third term in the decomposition captures the effect of different price regimes on the growth or decline of firms that have different time T decision rules. Again, under a variety of assumptions, selection effects will be standard. One can prove that this is the case, for example, if along-the-rule and search responses occur very rapidly so that, in effect, capital stock can be considered constant while these changes are going on, and if firm growth rates are linearly related to their profit rates.

Thus, models within an evolutionary theory are quite capable of explaining and predicting, the standard kind of responses of firms and industries to changes in market conditions. Further, I propose that, while somewhat more complicated, the richer formulation provided by an evolutionary theory corresponds much better to what economists' really believe, their 'appreciative' theory about what happens, than does the neo-classical formulation.

For example, consider analysis of the effects of the rise of oil prices in the 1970s. Most economists recognize that most firms did not have premade plans for coping with a large jump in oil prices. While a few did – notably certain public utilities that in the past had the practice of switching among alternative fuel sources in response to changes in prices – for most this was a situation not faced before, and not thought about much. Not all firms would be equally successful in thinking through what to do, or in doing R and D to discover or create ways to substitute or conserve. Part of the process of responding thus would involve induced innovation, and part a winnowing out of firms on the basis of who coped effectively and who did not. This relatively complex verbal story is not well-abstracted in terms of 'picking a different point along an isoquant'. Models within an evolutionary theory come much closer to characterizing it.

(C) Productivity growth fueled by technical advance

Earlier I recounted the renaissance in the 1950s of economists' interest in productivity growth fueled by technical advance. The theoretical framework used to analyze the phenomena in question was basically built from the intellectual tool kit of static microeconomic analysis. The models employed were virtually identical in spirit to those in the standard price theory text with two accommodations to the different task. Factors of production, particularly capital, were seen as growing over time. Technical advance, in the form of a 'shift' in the production function, was allowed. But the basic neo-classical analytic structure was preserved in the new growth models.

That would not be a problem if what scholars learned about technical change turned out to be consistent with the basic assumptions of the model. I have stressed that this was not the case. Technical change is not adequately treated in a model that assumes continuing profit maximizing equilibrium. While the neo-classical model is able to track the aggregative variables, it is flatly inconsistent with the actual processes. This weakness of neo-classical theory shows up when one looks at microeconomic data. For example, intrasectorial data display a considerable variation across firms in input coefficients, total factor productivity, and profitability. Also, beneath the relatively smooth movements of the macroaggregates one can see more turbulent motion, some revealed by diffusion studies of the spread of particular innovations displacing older technologies, some reflected in the rise or fall of particular firms. The challenge for an evolutionary model is to be as good as (maybe better than) a neo-classical one in dealing with aggregates, but to be more consistent with (perhaps even explain) the micro patterns. Much of my early work with Sidney Winter was aimed at achieving just these objectives.[3]

The model we employed contained the following elements. All feasible 'techniques' are assumed to be of the Leontief variety, employing a fixed amount of labor and a fixed amount of capital per unit of output. Each firm's output rule is always to operate at full capacity. Its investment rule is, essentially, to plow back all profits net of required dividends into gross investment (prevailing capital stocks

[3] Nelson and Winter (1974). A revised version is contained in Chapters 8 and 9 of Nelson and Winter (1982a).

were subject to depreciation). Firms engage in two different kinds of 'search'. One kind, which we called 'internal' search, involves their sampling of the population of feasible techniques. Search is 'local' in the sense that a firm is more likely to find a technique 'close' to its current technique than one that is far away. The other kind of search involves looking at what competitive firms are doing. If a newly found technique is more profitable than the prevailing technique, a firm switches over all its capital to the new technique. In so doing it establishes a new starting place for future local search. The context is a macro economy with Say's law assumed. At any time the economy faces an upward sloping labor supply curve; over time this curve shifts to the right as the labor supply grows. Growth of capital is, of course, endogenous to the analysis.

This model has the Markovian structure of most of our evolutionary models. Start the system with a number of firms, each with a capital stock, and each possessing a particular technique. The 'operate at capacity' rule determines, for each firm and for the economy, output and employment. The labor supply curve then is consulted to determine the wage rate. The net 'profit' of each of the firms is simply output minus the wage bill minus required dividends. (Output price is the numeraire.) Next period's capital stocks then are generated. Firms probabilistically find new techniques through search. If they come up with one that is more profitable than the one they have, they switch over to it. The techniques associated with each firm's next period then are determined. The labor supply curve shifts to the right. The process begins anew.

As noted earlier, Robert Solow's 'Technical Change and the Aggregate Production Function' set the style of laying on a neo-classical explanation for observed macro growth patterns. Since we wanted to draw a contrast between neo-classical and evolutionary explanations, we addressed the same data as did Solow, the macro time series of GNP, labor input, capital stock, and factor prices and shares, from 1909 to 1949. We set initial conditions of our model so that the overall constellation was roughly 'right' for the year 1909. We then ran the model for 40 periods, the length of time Solow explored. We did this in a large number of runs, varying a number of the key model parameters. We aimed to get a set of parameters which tracked the real data reasonably well, but in no way did we try to get a 'best' fit.

Some of our time paths were way off, others fit the data quite well. It turned out to be relatively easy to set up the model so that the macro time path generated by it would reveal a rising output per worker, rising capital labor ratio, a rising wage rate, and a roughly constant rate of return on capital and share of capital in total income. Table 1 presents data from one of our simulations, and the actual data addressed by Solow.

Regarding the macro data, we think the contest should be regarded a 'tie'. The time paths of the central macroeconomic variables are explained as well by an evolutionary model as by a neo-classical one. An econometrician looking at the macro data generated by virtually any of our runs would have difficulty in rejecting the hypothesis (Solow's) that the time series were generated by a Cobb–Douglas, neutral technical change process, although they obviously were not.

Table 1

Selected time series from simulation run 0001, compared with Solow data, 1909–1949.

Year	Q/L Sim.	Q/L Solow	K/L Sim.	K/L Solow	W Sim.	W Solow	S_A Sim.	S_A Solow	A Sim.	A Solow
1909	0.66	0.73	1.85	2.06	0.51	0.49	0.23	0.34	1.000	1.000
1910	0.68	0.72	1.84	2.10	0.54	0.48	0.21	0.33	1.020	0.933
1911	0.69	0.76	1.83	2.17	0.52	0.50	0.25	0.34	1.040	1.021
1912	0.71	0.76	1.91	2.21	0.50	0.51	0.30	0.33	1.059	1.023
1913	0.74	0.80	1.94	2.23	0.51	0.53	0.31	0.33	1.096	1.054
1914	0.72	0.80	1.86	2.20	0.61	0.54	0.15	0.33	1.087	1.071
1915	0.74	0.78	1.89	2.26	0.56	0.51	0.24	0.34	1.103	1.041
1916	0.76	0.82	1.89	2.34	0.60	0.53	0.21	0.36	1.136	1.076
1917	0.78	0.80	1.93	2.21	0.59	0.50	0.23	0.37	1.159	1.005
1918	0.78	0.85	1.90	2.22	0.62	0.56	0.21	0.34	1.169	1.142
1919	0.80	0.90	1.96	2.47	0.57	0.53	0.29	0.35	1.199	1.157
1920	0.80	0.84	1.94	2.58	0.64	0.58	0.19	0.32	1.192	1.069
1921	0.81	0.90	2.00	2.55	0.61	0.57	0.25	0.37	1.208	1.116
1922	0.83	0.92	2.02	2.49	0.65	0.61	0.21	0.34	1.225	1.183
1923	0.83	0.95	1.97	2.61	0.70	0.63	0.17	0.34	1.243	1.126
1924	0.86	0.98	2.05	2.74	0.64	0.66	0.25	0.33	1.274	1.245
1925	0.89	1.02	2.19	2.81	0.59	0.68	0.33	0.34	1.293	1.254
1926	0.87	1.02	2.07	2.87	0.74	0.63	0.15	0.33	1.288	1.244
1927	0.90	1.02	2.16	2.93	0.67	0.69	0.25	0.32	1.324	1.235
1928	0.91	1.02	2.18	3.62	0.70	0.68	0.23	0.34	1.336	1.226
1929	0.94	1.05	2.27	3.06	0.68	0.70	0.28	0.33	1.370	1.251
1930	0.93	1.03	2.47	3.30	0.62	0.67	0.37	0.35	1.394	1.197
1931	0.49	1.06	2.46	3.38	0.70	0.71	0.29	0.33	1.403	1.226
1932	1.62	1.03	2.57	3.28	0.69	0.62	0.32	0.40	1.435	1.108
1933	1.02	1.02	2.46	3.40	0.85	0.65	0.46	0.36	1.452	1.214
1934	1.04	1.08	2.45	3.00	0.85	0.70	0.19	0.36	1.486	1.298
1935	1.05	1.10	2.44	2.87	0.87	0.72	0.17	0.35	1.500	1.349
1936	1.06	1.15	2.51	2.72	0.82	0.74	0.22	0.36	1.499	1.429
1937	1.06	1.14	2.55	2.71	0.83	0.75	0.22	0.34	1.500	1.415
1938	1.11	1.17	2.74	2.78	0.76	0.73	0.32	0.33	1.543	1.445
1939	1.10	1.21	2.66	2.66	0.88	0.79	0.20	0.35	1.540	1.514
1940	1.13	1.27	2.75	2.63	0.84	0.82	0.25	0.36	1.576	1.590

Table 1 (continued).

Year	Q/L		K/L		W		S_A		A	
	Sim.	Solow	Sim.	Solow	Sim.	Solow	Sim.	Solow	Sim.	Solow
1941	1.16	1.31	2.77	2.58	0.90	0.82	0.23	0.38	1.618	1.660
1942	1.18	1.33	2.78	2.64	0.95	0.86	0.20	0.36	1.641	1.665
1943	1.49	1.38	2.79	2.62	0.93	0.91	0.22	0.34	1.652	1.733
1944	1.20	1.48	2.80	2.63	0.97	0.99	0.20	0.33	1.672	1.856
1945	1.21	1.52	2.82	2.66	0.97	1.04	0.20	0.31	1.683	1.895
1946	1.23	1.42	2.88	2.50	0.96	0.93	0.22	0.31	1.694	1.842
1947	1.23	1.40	2.89	2.50	0.93	0.94	0.21	0.33	1.701	1.791
1948	1.23	1.43	2.87	2.55	1.01	0.95	0.18	0.33	1.698	1.809
1949	1.23	1.49	2.82	2.70	1.04	1.01	0.15	0.33	1.703	1.852

Q/L Output (1929 dollars per man-hour; Solow data adjusted from 1939 to 1929 dollars by multiplying by 1.171 = ratio of implicit price deflators for GNP).

K/L Capital (1929 dollars per man-hour).

W Wage rate (1929 dollars per man-hour; Solow data adjusted from 1939 to 1929 dollars).

S_A Capital share (= 1 - labour share).

A Solow technology index. (Recalculation on the basis of figures in other columns will not check exactly, because of rounding of those figures. Solow figures shown for 1944–1949 are correct; the values originally published were in error.)

We think, however, our model provides a more plausible explanation of the macro time paths than the Cobb–Douglas model. Once the parameters (basic institutions?) are set in a way that encourages capital to grow faster than the labor supply, in our model, as in the orthodox one, wage rates rise. In our model, as in the orthodox one, rising wage rates make previously unprofitable capital intensive techniques profitable to adopt, and make unprofitable labor intensive techniques which used to be profitable. Innovation is nudged in a labor saving direction, and the capital labor ratio and output per worker rise. This is the neo-classical account also, but with our theory we are able to express the logic without assuming maximization or equilibrium; we need assume only profit oriented calculating behavior and competitive selection pressure. It's a much more plausible story.

Even if the contest were viewed as a tie at the macro level, at the micro level there is no contest. As stated, many of the microeconomic observations about technical change and related phenomena are flatly inconsistent with the standard formulation, even when it is doctored to admit things like different vintages of capital. Our model generated distributions across firms of variables like productivity levels, and sizes. The productivity distributions are reminiscent of those published by the BLS and studied some time ago by Salter. I propose that they are much more consistent with the mechanisms assumed in our model, than in his. The distribution of firm sizes generated by the model also is reminiscent of actual empirical observations.

Our model produced data on the spread of new techniques among the firms. The shapes of these 'diffusion' curves were similar to those found by scholars studying diffusion except that in most cases the use of a technique eventually began to fall off as still newer techniques superseded it.

Thus, our account of economic growth and technical change is simultaneously consistent with both, in quantitative terms, the broad features of macro time series, and, qualitatively, such microeconomic phenomena as cross section dispersions in capital labor ratios and efficiency, and patterns of diffusion of techniques. While the neo-classical account can track macro data, it is flatly inconsistent with the microeconomic phenomena associated with technical change.

(D) Modeling competition in the sense of Schumpeter

Virtually all economists agree that, for many sectors of the economy, Schumpeter's characterization of competition seems much more salient than the view presented in neoclassical textbooks. In electronics, pharmaceuticals and many other industries, without playing down the role of pricing strategies and wars, it is plain that competition among firms centrally involves their R and D policies, successes and failures. And, as Schumpeter stressed, over the long run the gains to society from continuing innovation are vastly greater than those associated with competitive pricing.

In articulating this view of competition, Schumpeter also put forth what has been called the 'Schumpeterian hypothesis' that a market structure involving firms, each with a considerable degree of market power, is the price that society must pay for rapid technological advance. Thus, there is a trade-off between static efficiency, in the sense of prices close to marginal production cost, and dynamic progressiveness. It is not clear how much choice Schumpeter thought society actually had regarding the mix between static efficiency and dynamic progressivity, but many contemporary economists clearly write as if they think that market structure is a variable potentially under tight public control.

I would like to distinguish between Schumpeter's general propositions about the nature and social value of competition in technically progressive industries, and his specific hypothesis about market structure and technical change. One can accept the right-headedness of the former while remaining open-minded or skeptical about the latter. And in the last few decades there has been a rash of theoretical models, as well as empirical studies, exploring the connections between market structure and technical progress. These turn out to be considerably more complicated than at least the simple version of the 'Schumpeterian hypothesis'.

Most of the modeling of Schumpeterian competition has rested on the neo-classical assumption of maximization and equilibrium, sometimes interpreted in terms of a dynamic game. However, for the reasons espoused earlier, maximization and equilibrium do not seem appropriate assumptions for modeling contests involving innovation. In Schumpeterian competition there are winners and losers, and it is unlikely to be clear before the fact which player will be first, or last. Winning is partly a matter of having a good strategy. But it is not easy to judge, ex ante, what the best strategies are likely to be. Different firms make different bets. Only the actual experience will tell who bet right or wrong. One cannot adequately explore the process with a model that assumes the contest is over and has resulted in a tie.

Once one thinks about Schumpeterian competition from the viewpoint of evolutionary theory, it is plain that the causal connections between technical change and market structure flow both ways. Large firms may or may not be good at innovation, but firms that are good at innovation will tend to be profitable, to grow, and to become large. If both luck and size contribute to innovation, there is the possibility here for competition to self-destruct as a successful innovator comes to dominate the industry. On the other hand, if innovation is costly and imitation relatively easy, firms that try to innovate may be able to survive only if they are large. There clearly are a rich set of dynamic possibilities here which cannot possibly be attacked with orthodox tools.

Winter and I have attempted to attack them with a model similar in many respects to the one discussed in the preceding section, but tailored for analysis of Schumpeterian competition. The principal differences between the present model and the former one are as follows.[4] First, differences among techniques in the capital labor ratio are repressed, and techniques are assumed to differ only in their 'total efficiency'. Efficiency is defined in terms of output per unit of capital. Second, the R and D policies tie their R and D spending to their size. The size of a firm's R and D budget determines the probability that a firm will find an element in the urn where it is searching. Thus, large firms, who spend more on R and D, have a greater chance of successfully drawing from the relevant distributions. Third, in contrast with the model of the previous section, in the one discussed here investment of a firm is linked not only to its profits, but to its market share. Unlike small firms, firms whose sales account for a significant fraction of the market may hold back their own growth to avoid spoiling the market. Fourth, this is a 'sectorial' model, with a downward sloping demand curve,

---

[4] Nelson and Winter (1977, 1980, 1982b). These models appear in revised form in Nelson and Winter (1982a, chs. 12,13,14).

and the wage rate is exogenous.

The following simplifies in certain respects from our actual simulation model, but displays the basic logic.

$$Q_{it} = A_{it} K_{it}. \tag{6}$$

The output of firm i at time t equals its capital stock times the productivity of the technique it is using.

$$P_t = D\Sigma (Q_{it}). \tag{7}$$

$$\pi_{it} = P_t A_{it} - c - r_i. \tag{8}$$

The profit on capital equals revenues minus production costs associated with production inputs, minus R and D costs, all per unit of capital.

$$K_i (t+1) = I \left(\pi_{it}, \frac{Q_{it}}{\Sigma Q_{it}} \right) K_{it}. \tag{9}$$

The relative growth, or decline, of a firm's capital is determined by its profit rate and its market shares.

$$\text{Pr (draw} = 1) = ar_i K_{it}. \tag{10}$$

The probability that a firm will get a 'draw' from a relevant population of alternative technologies is proportional to its total R and D spending. The populations drawn from include that defined by the 'technological opportunities' facing the firm (which we specify in several different ways), and that defined by the technologies employed by other firms. For a firm that has both an imitation draw, A^m, and an innovation draw, A^n, the productivity level next period is given by

$$A_i\,(t+1) \;=\; \max\,(A_{it},\,A^m{}_{it},\,A^n{}_{it}). \tag{11}$$

Such a model is well designed to examine the conditions under which competition will and won't tend to self-destruct. In our model, at least, three factors make an important difference. First, the magnitude of the efficiency edge that the average innovation yields the innovating firm over its competitors. Second, the ease or difficulty of imitation, in the sense of the expected amount of R and D resources that need to be applied before a successful innovation of one firm can be copied by another. Third, the extent to which profitable large firms continue to press their advantage through further growth. In circumstances where innovation does not give a major advantage, and imitation is relatively easy, an initial competitive structure tends to be preserved. In contrast, where significant advantages go to the innovator, imitation is hard and investment behavior aggressive, there is a high likelihood that a dominant firm will emerge.

Once a firm with a superior technology comes to account for a large share of the industry's output, the competitive fringe is unlikely to recover, within this model at least. In competition against the dominant firm, small firms are disadvantaged because of their smaller R and D spending. If a small firm comes up with a profitable innovation, that firm can expect only a limited time before the dominant firm copies its new techniques or comes up with something better. Limits on a firm's growth rate mean that, in that sheltered interval, the smaller innovator is likely to be able to make up only a small portion of its size, and R and D spending, disadvantage.

In the model summarized above, we assumed that all firms spend both on R and D aimed at innovation and R and D aimed at imitation. In another model in the same family we assumed that some firms chose to spend both on innovative and imitative R and D, and others only on imitative R and D. The natural question then arises – under what conditions will the innovators thrive and prosper, and under what conditions will innovation be driven from the industry? The above discussion suggests that this depends on whether innovation, if achieved, is likely to give a significant advantage, and on how costly it is to imitate an innovation. Where a successful innovation is likely to give only a small advantage, and imitation is relatively easy, innovators do not fare well. While imitators tend to lag somewhat technologically this is not a serious penalty, and often is more than offset by the fact that they spend less on R and D. Where large profitable imitators were aggressive in their investment behavior, innovators tend to be forced out of the industry.

What differences does this make for the overall productivity growth of the industry? Of course, this ought to depend on the relationship between innovative R and D spending in the industry, and the overall rate of technical advance in the industry. One can think of several different possibilities. One is that innovative R and D in the industry consists largely of exploiting new ideas created by outside science, or making use of a flow of new materials and components created by supplying industries. In this case low innovative R and D in the industry itself would result in a jerkier time path of best practice and a somewhat lower overall track than were internal innovation oriented R and D higher, but not necessarily a lower rate of growth of productivity. On the other hand, if technical change in the industry results largely from its own internal R and D and today's R and D efforts build on yesterday's R and D successes, a lower internal R and D spending might be expected to translate into a slower rate of advance of best and average practice technology.

Our models of Schumpeterian competition tend to confirm these conjectures. Or, rather, working with our models made us think about them. Whereas Schumpeterian competition has proved very difficult terrain to explore with models built along orthodox lines, the subject seems to be natural turf for the implementation of ideas drawn from evolutionary theory.

(E) A model of coexistence of innovators and imitators

As my final example, I present a model of dynamic equilibrium, in which firms that innovate and firms that imitate coexist. Such a model turns out to provide a reason for expecting a positive relationship in the cross section between an industry's rate of technical progress and the R and D intensity in that industry, that differs in interesting respects from the rationale provided by neo-classical theory.

Assume, as in the last model, that a firm that invests in innovative R and D gets, as a result, a technological edge over a firm that does not, but that firms that do not try to innovate can spend less on R and D and can imitate, with a lag, the innovator's technology. Assume that a firm's R and

D strategy is defined as an R and D to sales ratio, with imitators having a ratio δ times that of innovators, and adapting the innovator's technology with a lag of L years. Ignore stochastic elements. What are the conditions under which innovators and imitators will have the same total costs per unit of output, inducting R and D as well as production costs?

Let $\Delta A/A$ be the rate at which innovators reduce their unit production costs from their R and D. Then innovators and imitators will have the same total costs per unit of output when

$$\left(\frac{R}{S}\right)_{IN} P + C_{IN} = \delta \left(\frac{R}{S}\right)_{IN} P$$
$$+ \left(1 + \frac{\Delta A}{A} \cdot L\right) C_{IN}. \quad (12)$$

The left-hand side shows R and D costs plus production costs per unit of output for the innovators, the right-hand side for the imitators.

This equation ties together $\Delta A/A$ and $(R/S)_{IN}$ in an interesting way.

$$\frac{\Delta A}{A} = \left(\frac{R}{S}\right)_{IN} \frac{(1-\delta)}{L} \cdot \frac{P}{C_{IN}}. \quad (13)$$

Alternatively,

$$\frac{R}{S_{IN}} = \frac{\Delta A}{A} \left(\frac{L}{1-\delta}\right) \cdot \frac{C_{IN}}{P}. \quad (14)$$

One could try to squeeze something out of the way the price–cost margin enters these equations. Thus, making the Cournot assumption about output determination, one might say that eq. (13) suggests that, other things (δ and L) being equal, a given R and D intensity of innovators is associated with more rapid technological advance when the innovating firms have considerable market power, than when they do not. Alternatively, one might argue that P/C_{IN} is likely to be close enough to unity to be ignored in the analysis.

Eqs. (13) and (14) indicate that, given $L/(1-\delta)$, high total factor productivity growth and high research intensity should go together. However, eq. (13) alerts us to the fact that R and D intensity can be high even where technical progress is slow, if $L/(1-\delta)$ (a measure of the ability of innovators to reap returns from their R and D) is high. Thus, in contemplating eq. (13), one ought to recognize that R/S, and $(1-\delta)/L$, are likely to be negatively correlated. Nonetheless, unless this correlation is very strong, one would expect to see $\Delta A/A$, and R/S, positively correlated in the cross section of industries. We have thus arrived at a familiar hypothesis, but through a chain of analysis tied to evolutionary, not neo-classical, theory.

However, the analysis suggests that the R and D intensity in an industry that is most likely to be correlated with industry productivity growth is the R and D to sales ratios of firms near the frontier, not necessarily the average R and D intensity in the industry. While, in some industries, the R and D policies of most firms tend to be similar, in other industries there are noticeable differences, with some firms aiming to be innovative, and others earning their living by imitating with a lag, but spending less on R and D. This latter group drags down average industry R and D intensity. However, it is the presence of the former group that signals that R and D is productive.

Chapter 3

INTER-INDUSTRY DIFFERENCES

In Chapter 2 I mentioned, but did not highlight, inter-industry differences. In fact, there are major differences across industries in terms of measured rates of technical progress, research and development intensity, and, as we shall see, a number of other variables which reflect or bear on technical progress.

(A) How to explain the differences?

Economists have long been aware of significant inter-industry differences in rates of growth of labor productivity. During the late 1950s, largely as a result of the work of John Kendrick, data on total factor productivity growth at the level of individual industries became available.[1] Cross industry variation in growth of total factor productivity turned out to be almost as large as cross industry variation in growth of labor productivity, and to be strongly correlated. While scholars recognized that many factors might lie behind these differences, it seemed plausible that to a considerable extent they reflected cross industry differences in rates of technical advance. This interpretation was lent added credibility by the fact that in a number of industries experiencing rapid total factor productivity growth, signifi-

[1] The key publication was Kendrick (1961).

cant technical advances obviously were occurring. Still further support was provided by Terleckyj's research, reported in the Kendrick study, which showed a significant positive relationship between an industry's growth rate of total factor productivity, and its R and D intensity (R and D divided by value added). Thus by the late 1950s the following string of causation was widely believed. Inter-industry differences in growth of output per worker are largely the result of differences in rates of growth of total factor productivity, which were associated with rates of technical progress in that industry; in turn, industry technical progress is determined in part at least by the R and D intensity of the industry.

Since that time a considerable amount of research has been directed toward refining and elaborating the basic model. Scholars have sought to refine and elaborate measures of R and D input relevant to technical change in an industry. That part of R and D done in an industry financed privately has been separated from government financed R and D, and applied R and D has been separated from basic research done in an industry.

By and large multiple regressions show that, while private R and D intensity is positively related to total factor productivity growth, government financed R and D is not.[2] However, almost all government industrial R and D financing is concentrated in the very few industries from which the government procures major weapons and space systems or subsystems. Existing price measures fail to capture increased

---

[2] See, for example, Terleckyj (1980).

product performance in these industries, and hence total factor productivity growth, as presently measured, accounts poorly for the technical advances bought by government. In other fields where microeconomic studies suggest a significant positive effect of government financed R and D, like the industries associated with agriculture, the publicly funded R and D is conducted in government or university laboratories, and not by the firms in the industry in question. This kind of publicly financed R and D spending is thus missed in the regression.

In some multiple regression studies, basic research done in an industry has been calculated to be associated with a larger effect, per marginal dollar, than applied R and D. However, it seems plausible that industries that spend a lot on basic research do so in large part because the scientific understanding of their technologies is already strong. Thus, according to this view, industrial basic research spending is largely the consequence of certain underlying factors that facilitate technical advance, rather than an independent factor in its own right.

A number of studies have considered the effect of R and D done by upstream industries – producers of capital equipment and materials – as well as an industry's own R and D, on its rate of productivity growth.[3] The effects of upstream R and D generally turn out to be large. Some such 'pass on' is not surprising, and clearly is of analytic significance. Where the pass on is large, I suspect that what is happening is that the R and D done in an upstream industry is gener-

[3] Terleckyj (1980).

ating technical improvements that are not getting measured adequately in its own output statistics because actual or potential competition does not permit the price of the new machine or material to reflect its full advantages over its predecessors.

In any case, it is now quite well documented that industries that experience rapid sustained technical progress, as measured by the rate of growth of total factor productivity, are characterized by high research and development intensity of the firms in the industry, or of upstream firms, or both. However, this only kicks the puzzle one stage back. What lies behind the very considerable observed differences in R and D intensities across industries?

The broad view of technical advance provided by evolutionary theory, and the sharper but more stylized insights that can be drawn from particular formal models, suggest the kinds of factors that may be operative behind the scenes. Consider, for example, the last two models discussed in the preceding chapter, in which conditions conducive to, and threatening for, the survivability of innovating firms were studied. Survivability of the innovators depended on innovative R and D being productive. Something significant had to come out of the investment. This was necessary, but not sufficient. In addition, imitation must not be too quick or too cheap. Innovators must be able to appropriate a significant share of the returns from the R and D that they do, at least for a reasonable period of time.

(B) The survey research study of technological opportunity and appropriability

Since technological opportunity and ability to appropriate returns are such important variables within evolutionary theory my colleagues and I were drawn to undertake empirical research to get a better fix on them. To that end, we designed a questionnaire, which ultimately was sent out to nearly 1,000 R and D executives.[4] We ultimately received and can work with 650 completed questionnaires. There are 130 lines of business represented among these. Obviously, then, we have more than one response for a number of lines of business. Given the way our list of addresses was drawn up, in general we have several responses from industries that are R and D intensive.

Our strategy for dealing with the measurement problem was to ask our respondents to score their answer to a particular question on a seven point semantic scale (for example, we asked our respondents to pick a number between one and seven as their appraisal of the effectiveness of patents). We use the responses both to assess cross industry differences (for example, in the effectiveness of patents), and intra-industry differences (for example, whether patents are or are not more effective than secrecy). We are well aware of the problematic nature of these comparisons. However, we have built some cross-checks into the questionnaire, and it is possible also in some cases to compare the numbers we ob-

---

[4] We describe the questionnaire and report preliminary findings in Levin et al. (1984).

tained from the questionnaire with other numbers. Without further ado, I give some highlights on what the questionnaire has revealed.

Appropriability. In the last two models discussed in Chapter 2, while conditions of appropriability clearly played a central role, there was no specification of the means through which a firm reaped returns from its innovations, and held off other firms from eating too much and too rapidly into those returns. There has been only a limited amount of research on that subject, and virtually all of that has been concerned with the importance of patents in different industries. Here, Scherer, Taylor and Silberston, and Mansfield and colleagues, all have done important work, showing that the range of industries where patents are effective may be quite limited.[5] However, effective patent protection may not be necessary for a firm to be able to appropriate a significant fraction of the returns from its innovation. Scholars writing about the semi-conductor, and computer, industries have stressed the importance of lead time and learning curve advantages, in rewarding an innovator. It is well known that in some industries firms try to protect their innovations, particularly of new processes, through keeping them secret. Our questionnaire was designed to explore what means of appropriating returns to innovation are effective in different industries, and to assess interindustry differences in the ability of innovators to reap returns through any instrument or package of them.

---

[5] Scherer (1959), Taylor and Silberston (1973), Mansfield et al. (1981).

Thus, we asked our respondents the following question: 'In this line of business how effective is each of the following means of capturing and protecting the competitive advantages of new or improved products?' The listed means were: (1) patents to prevent competitors from duplicating the product, (2) patents to secure royalty income, (3) secrecy, (4) lead time, (5) moving quickly down the learning curve, and, (6) superior sales or service efforts. We requested our respondents to circle a number from one to seven for each of the means, where one was labeled 'not at all effective' and seven was labeled 'very effective'. We asked an identical set of questions about the effectiveness of various means for appropriating the returns to process innovations.

Figures 1 and 2 display the pattern of responses. These figures provide for each question a bar graph that divides the responses from the lines of business in our sample into quintiles. For example, Figure 1 shows that respondents in one-fifth of the industries rated the effectiveness of patents to prevent duplication of new or improved products at five or greater, another fifth rated effectiveness between 4.3 and 5.0, but that one-fifth of the respondents rated patent effectiveness at 3.0 or less. An examination of Figure 1 shows that, on average, our respondents rated lead time, moving quickly down the learning curve, and superior sales or service effects, as significantly more effective in protecting new products in their line of business than patents to prevent duplication, or to secure royalty income. On average, secrecy was less effective than patent protection.

There are interesting differences between the responses for process innovation and product innovation. As a general

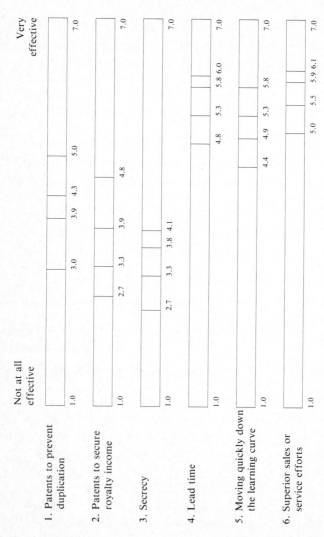

Figure 1. Effectiveness of alternative means of protecting the competitive advantage of new or improved production products (responses displayed by quintiles).

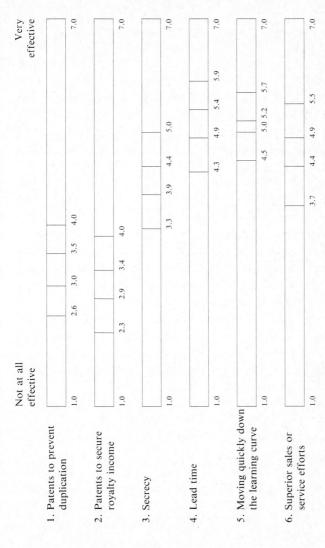

Figure 2. Effectiveness of alternative means of protecting the competitive advantage of new or improved production processes (responses displayed by quintiles).

rule, it seems that most means of protecting proprietary interests, for example patents, are weaker for process innovation than for product innovation. However, secrecy is more effective. The lesser ability to protect a process with a patent, and the greater ability to protect through secrecy, are opposite sides of the same coin. One gains profit from one's new products by getting them out into the market for other people to buy and use. This makes secrecy about product design difficult or impossible. However, if a competitor were to steal the innovator's product technology and produce a comparable product, that would be visible. If one had a patent one believed would hold up in court, one knows whom to sue. On the other hand, a firm often can gain advantage from its process innovations, which reduce its production costs, or enhance the quality of its products, without divulging its process technology through the products it sells. Thus secrecy is a viable option. However, a competitor who somehow or other finds out about the innovator's process innovation, may be able to adopt it without the innovating firm having any clear evidence that it has. Under such a circumstance, the fact that the innovator has a patent may be meaningless.

Perhaps the most striking feature of Figures 1 and 2 is the great inter-industry diversity they show. While many industries rate patent protection on new products as quite ineffective, 25 of our 130 industries rated the effectiveness of product patents above five. Almost all of these industries fit into one or another of two groups. One consists of industries producing chemical products or close relatives (inorganic chemicals, plastic materials, synthetic fibers, synthetic rubber, and glass). The other consists of industries producing relatively uncomplicated mechanical equipment (air and gas compressors, power driven handtools, etcetera). In both of these cases, the composition of the products is relatively easy to define and to delimit, and apparently under these conditions patents seem to be effective.

As Figure 1 shows, a significantly larger number of industries rated the effectiveness of lead time, or rapidly moving down the learning curve, at five or greater. Included here are such industries as semi-conductors, computers and aircraft. For semi-conductors, product patents also were judged to be relatively effective in protecting proprietary new products, but not so in computers or aircraft.

It is apparent that the various means of protecting innovation do not operate independently. Where patents were judged effective in preventing duplication, they also tended to be rated effective in securing royalty income. Similarly, the effectiveness of lead time, and moving quickly down the learning curve, were strongly positively correlated. For product innovation, these two instrumentalities also were positively correlated with superior sales or service efforts. For process innovation they were positively correlated with the effectiveness score for secrecy.

Are there two different clusters of appropriability mechanisms that are quite different in terms of how they work? We have some evidence that suggests this is so. Patents enhance appropriability by increasing imitation costs and lags. Head start and learning curve advantages stem from running away from the pack.

We asked our respondents about the cost and time it

would take for a competent firm to imitate the innovation of
a competitor when the innovation was patented, and when
it was not. The differences can be interpreted as indirect
measures of patent effectiveness. The difference made by the
presence of a patent, so measured, varied significantly across
industries. And there is a strong positive correlation between
rated patent effectiveness in an industry, as scored by our
direct question, and the reported increase in imitation cost
and time, associated with the presence of a patent. On the
other hand, the cost and time required for duplication,
whether the innovation is patented or not, do not seem to be
linked strongly to the rated effectiveness of lead time, or of
learning curve advantages, in enabling an innovator to reap
returns. Apparently the effectiveness of these mechanisms is
associated with major gains from getting in first and having
a temporary monopoly for a short period of time, rather
than from holding off imitators for a long period of time.

Given that there are significant inter-industry differences
in the means, or packages of means, that are most effective
in enabling an innovating firm to seize returns, what kind of
summary measures seem plausible to characterize appropriability conditions in an industry? The hypothesis that
I and my colleagues like most is that it only takes one really
effective means to enable a firm to appropriate returns. By
this measure, nearly 80 of our 130 industries gave at least
one instrument a score of six or greater regarding effectiveness in protecting product innovation. Nine industries
scored no instrument as more effective than five. This latter
group consisted largely of food processing and metal working industries.

In contrast, less than 50 industries rated their most effective instrument for reaping returns on a process innovation at six or greater. Thirty-five gave their most effective means for protecting process innovation a score of five, or less.

The fact that product innovations tend to be significantly easier to protect than process innovations does not necessarily imply that there are no incentives for someone, or some firm, to work on an industry's process technologies. Not always, but often, the effectiveness of an industry's processes depends on the character and quality of the material inputs it purchases, and the capital equipment it uses. But these are products of upstream industries. The fact that process innovations are more difficult to protect than product innovations has the consequence, therefore, of locating much of the work on the latter upstream.

Technological opportunity. Industries almost certainly differ in the effectiveness or productivity of their R and D investments, as well as in their ability to appropriate returns from them. Here I focus on one important source of such differences – strength of links with science.

Several scholars have described and analyzed the rise of industrial R and D in the United States and in Europe, toward the end of the 19th century, and observed that this institutional development was due largely to the advance of certain sciences that were highly relevant to certain industrial technologies.[6] The first industrial research

---

[6] See, for example, Noble (1977) and Rosenberg (1985).

laboratories were in companies producing chemical or electrical products, and the work in these laboratories rested heavily on new scientific understanding in chemistry and physics. Since those early days of industrial research and development, evolving scientific understanding has touched a wider range of industrial technologies, and, relatedly, the range of industries doing research and development has broadened considerably. However, measured rates of technical progress are quite uneven across industries, and several scholars of technical progress have proposed that an important factor behind these inter-industry differences is that the technologies of some industries are better illuminated by scientific understanding than are the technologies of others.

To begin to map out the nature and strength of industrial connections with science, I and my colleagues asked about the relevance of various fields of basic science and various fields of applied science, to technological progress in the respondent's line of business. The basic scientific fields were biology, chemistry, geology, mathematics, and physics. The fields of applied science were agricultural science, applied math and operations research, computer science, material science, medical science, and metallurgy. We asked our respondents to score relevance along a scale from one to seven.

Every field of science received a score of six or higher from at least a few industries. As one might have expected, however, many scientific fields were important to only a narrow group. Thus biology was scored at five or higher by only 14 industries, and geology by four. There were four broad fields – chemistry, material science, computer science, and metallurgy – that received scores of six or higher from over 30 industries (out of the 130). The first three of these fields received a score of five or higher from more than half the industries in the survey. With five the cutoff, physics and applied math now make it to the list of sciences scored as relevant at that level or higher by 30 or more industries. Table 1 reports, for each of the fields of science on our questionnaire, the number of industries giving that field a relevance score of five or greater.

In terms of what industries regarded what sciences as important, there are few surprises. Thus physics and mathematics were deemed important by the industries one might believe would report them as so – semi-conductors, communications equipment, measuring devices, but also

Table 1

Number of industries giving a field of science a relevance score of five or greater.

Biology	14
Chemistry	74
Geology	4
Math	30
Physics	44
Agricultural science	16
Applied math and operations research	32
Computer science	79
Materials science	99
Medical science	8
Metallurgy	60

aircraft, guided missiles, pumps, and primary aluminum. Most of these industries, but not all, also reported high relevance for computer science and material science. The biological sciences and medical sciences also are rated as important by the industries one intuitively understands as being closely connected with them – drugs, surgical instruments, and perfumes and cosmetics. Chemistry was judged important by the industries generally deemed as employing chemistry based technologies – drugs, organic chemicals, plastics, petroleum refining, pulp and paper. Chemistry based industries also tend to report high relevance for material science, metallurgy, and computer science.

In view of the significant differences across industries regarding the fields of science that are relevant to them, it is not obvious how one goes about constructing a general measure of the closeness of an industry to science. My colleagues and I constructed two measures. One is the relevance score of the science rated most relevant by the industry in question. We also constructed a measure consisting of the sum of relevance scores across the various fields of science. Table 2 presents the rank ordering, from low to high, of the industries where we had ten or more responses, by these two criteria.

There obviously is positive correlation between these measures. By either, drugs and semi-conductors report themselves very close to science; and motors, generators and industrial controls, and motor vehicle parts and accessories, report some distance. However, there are some interesting differences between the two rank orderings. In particular,

Table 2

Ranked by largest relevance score	Ranked by sum of relevance scores
Motors, generators, and industrial controls	Motor vehicle parts and accessories
Motor vehicle parts and accessories	Motors, generators, and industrial controls
Pumps and pumping equipment	Perfumes, cosmetics, and toilet preparations
Measuring and controlling devices	Industrial organic chemicals
Industrial inorganic chemicals	Plastics, materials and resins
Perfumes, cosmetics, and toilet preparations	Pumps and pumping equipment
Pulp, paper, and paperboard mills	Communications equipment
Communications equipment	Plastic products
Aircraft and parts	Industrial inorganic chemicals
Industrial inorganic chemicals	Steelworks, rolling and finishing mills
Electronic computing equipment	Surgical and medical instruments
Steelworks, rolling and finishing mills	Electronic computing equipment
Plastic products	Aircraft and parts
Petroleum refining	Petroleum refining
Surgical and medical instruments	Drugs
Plastics, materials and resins	Pulp, paper, and paperboard mills
Semi-conductors and related devices	Measuring and controlling devices
Drugs	Semi-conductors and related devices

the chemistry based industries come out lower in the closeness ranking based on the sum of the relevance scores than on the ranking based on the largest relevance scores, suggesting that the scientific links of these industries while strong, are concentrated in a few fields.

Contribution from outside the industry.   We also asked a set of questions about the importance of the contribution of various outside sources to technical progress in different lines of business. Here we listed materials suppliers, suppliers of equipment used in manufacturing, suppliers of equipment used in research, users of the products of the industry, university research, government research laboratories, professional or technical societies, and independent inventors.

Of the list of outsiders, materials suppliers and suppliers of manufacturing equipment – upstream industries – were reported the most important, on average. More than 40 percent of the lines of business scored their contributions at five or greater. Suppliers of research equipment also were rated as very important by a number of different industries.

Nearly 30 respondents reported the contributions of users to technical advance in their line of business as greater than five. Included prominently in this list are industries making machinery for customers who are in a good position to do a lot of tinkering and advising. There also are a number of industries producing scientific or technical instruments where the users are highly sophisticated and, as shown by various studies, tend to do a reasonable amount of inventing on their own. Only eight industries rated the contribution of individual inventors as five or greater. However, half of these also showed up on the list of industries where the contribution of users was scored as five or greater.

The contribution of university research scored higher than five in only nine industries. With the exception of optical instruments and lenses, all of these were connected with health or with agriculture. Government laboratories were scored higher than five in only six industries. Included here are electron tubes, as well as optical instruments and lenses, and then as above, health and agricultural related industries.

(C) A regression analysis of the determinants of inventive efforts, and accomplishment

The data set we have gathered through our questionnaire is rich and intriguing, and I and my colleagues have only begun to analyze it. Thus, what I present to you now must be understood as very preliminary.

The determinants of R and D intensity. Table 3 presents *t* statistics from regressions for process R and D intensity, product R and D intensity, and total R and D intensity, fitted for a subpopulation of 43 industries for which we had five or more responses.[7] Product appropriability is a more important factor in the product R and D intensity regression than process appropriability is in the process R and D equation. On the other hand both the strength of links with

---

[7] Only *t* statistics are reported, since, in view of the metric used for independent variables, the coefficients themselves have no obvious meaning.

Table 3

t statistics from R and D intensity regressions.

	Process R and D intensity	Product R and D intensity	Total R and D intensity
Process appropriability	0.5		− 0.3
Product appropriability		1.8	1.6
Science links	3.2	0.7	1.6
C4	2.4	0.2	1.1
Contribution university research	1.4	1.2	1.4
Contribution professional societies	− 1.0	− 1.3	− 1.5
Contribution government research	− 1.6	0.9	0.4

science, and the concentration ratio, have more punch in the process R and D intensity equation. These relationships also obtain in regressions specified somewhat differently, or run on different subpopulations. We treated the reported contributions of university research, professional societies, and government research, as exogenous. The pattern shown in Table 3 of a positive relationship of R and D intensity with the contribution of university research, and a negative relation with the contribution of professional societies, shows up more strongly in regressions on other subpopulations.

Contributions by outsiders. Table 4 presents *t* statistics from regressions attempting to explain the contributions made by materials suppliers, equipment suppliers, research equipment suppliers, users and independent inventors. High

Table 4

t statistics from regressions on the contribution of outside sources.

	Contri-bution materials suppliers	Contri-bution equipment suppliers	Contri-bution research equipment suppliers	Contri-bution users	Contri-bution inde-pendent inventors
Process appropri-ability	1.5	1.4	0.7		1.4
Product appropri-ability				0.9	− 1.2
Science links	− 0.0	0.3	1.8	0.2	− 1.1
C4	− 0.7	− 0.0	− 0.4	− 1.0	− 2.6
Contribu-tion university research	0.3	− 0.4	2.4	− 0.4	2.1
Contribu-tion pro-fessional societies	2.5	2.0	− 0.2	− 0.2	0.6
Contribu-tion gov-ernment research	− 1.8	− 0.5	0.4	1.2	− 0.1

reported contribution of professional societies is strongly positively related to the reported contributions of upstream materials and equipment suppliers. This finding is robust and, in conjunction with the results reported in Table 3, suggests that there are two quite different structures supporting process innovation for an industry. If the industry is concentrated, it tends to spend a lot on process R and D itself. If it is unconcentrated, upstream firms are the principal sources, with professional societies playing a role tying together upstream and downstream expertise. Industry concentration also seems antithetical to a strong role of independent inventors. The strong positive association between the contribution of research equipment suppliers, and the contribution of university research, undoubtedly reflects that university researchers are an important source of research equipment inventions, which then get developed and sold by research equipment suppliers. The strong significance of the links with science variable in this equation likewise supports this interpretation.

To repeat, the results reported in Tables 3 and 4 are preliminary. My colleagues and I have only begun to explore these relationships. However, by and large the equations reported here provide an interesting and understandable picture of what supports, and what deters, R and D in the industry itself, and the contributions of upstream suppliers and private inventors.

New measures of technical change.   How well do the variables considered above explain differences across industries in rates of technical change? I examine this question below.

But first I want to describe the new measures of technical change we gathered through the questionnaire.

Growth of total factor productivity has certain well known liabilities when used as an index of the rate of technical change in an industry, especially when product attributes are changing rapidly. Also, total factor productivity growth measures are not available for all of the industries addressed in our questionnaire. Therefore, we asked our respondents to put down their subjective judgments about the pace at which new or improved production processes, and new or improved products, have been introduced in their line of business. Most respondents said that product innovation had been significantly faster than process innovation in their line of business. However, there was a strong positive correlation between the assessed rate of product and process innovation in a line of business.

The following industries rank at the top of the list in terms of the reported rate of both product and process innovation: radio and TV receiving sets, computers, semi-conductors, communications equipment, engineering and scientific instruments, and guided missiles. Primary aluminum and boiler shops rated toward the bottom of both lists. In general, the industries for which respondents reported rapid introduction of new products and processes tended to be the ones generally regarded as technologically progressive. The industries where new product and process introduction was reported as slow are ones that one commonly thinks of as having experienced little technical progress.

As a further check, we ran regressions of measured total

factor productivity growth, for the industries where such measures are available, against our reported product and process innovation rates in those industries. (In some cases we had to aggregate several of our lines of business to enable this procedure to go forward, in which case we used an average of the reported rates.) Our process innovation measure correlated quite strongly with total factor productivity growth. Not surprisingly, our product innovation measure correlated less well.

Factors associated with rapid technical advance. Table 5 presents *t* statistics from regressions for the reported rates of process and product innovation in an industry, and for their

Table 5

t statistics from regressions in rates of technical advances.

	Process innovation	Product innovation	Average innovation
Process R and D	2.0		
Product R and D		2.8	
Total R and D			3.4
Contribution materials suppliers	1.4	1.5	1.7
Contribution equipment suppliers	0.4	0.2	0.9
Contribution research equipment suppliers	1.5	1.7	1.5
Contribution users	2.4	2.8	2.7
Contribution independent inventors	1.1	1.1	1.2

average. The results are highly encouraging that the analysis is on track. Product and process innovation in an industry are strongly related to their relevant R and D intensities, and to the contributions of upstream and downstream outsiders.

Chapter 4

THE PUBLIC AND PRIVATE FACES OF TECHNOLOGY

(A) Trade-offs, and institutional assignments

In capitalist economies, technology has both a private and a public aspect. These complement each other, and are at odds.[1]

As I have stressed in the preceding chapter, it is proprietary rights that energize the capitalist system. Yet technology, or aspects of technology, has latent public good properties. To keep private a latent public good entails efficiency losses of various kinds. And, in fact, under capitalism many of these public good aspects are respected.

Both the private and the public aspects of technology are built into the patent system. Under patent law the lure and reward for invention is a temporary and limited legal right to control use of the invention. In exchange, the inventor discloses the invention and what makes it work, and agrees to abandon proprietary control after a certain number of years.

Both aspects of technology are built into the models of Schumpeterian competition described in Chapter 2. Schumpeter saw the lure and reward for innovation in

[1] Some of the material presented in this chapter was first presented at a conference on Innovation diffusion, held in Venice, Italy, in March 1986.

capitalist countries in the quasi-rents on the private temporary monopoly associated with the introduction of a new product or process. In the preceding chapter we examined a variety of mechanisms whereby quasi-rents are seized, and noted significant inter-industry differences. This is the private and proprietary side of the matter.

The public side reflects that, in Schumpeter's analysis and in our models, the monopoly normally is only temporary. The gains to an innovator are limited because, sooner or later, competitors will be able to imitate, or invent around, or develop a better version of, the initial innovation. The fact that technology ultimately goes public has three benefits. First, this assures that a healthy share of the benefits of an innovation goes to users and (in the parlance of economists) dead weight triangle costs of restriction are kept short-run and limited. Second, knowledge of the new innovation provides a base and a spur for further innovation by others. Third, by facilitating subsequent competition, the dangers that a company can build a wide and durable industry monopoly out of a series of innovations is kept under control.

Indeed, from one point of view, the job of institutional design is to get an appropriate balance of the private and public aspects of technology, enough private incentive to spur innovation, and enough publicness to facilitate wide use. Access to an innovation by competitors should not be so rapid or complete as to dull incentives to innovate. On the other hand, the stronger the restrictions on access and the longer their duration, the higher the social costs in terms of less than optimal use. Nordhaus and other scholars have examined trade-offs related to the duration of dead weight losses associated with patent length.[2] Sidney Winter and I have looked at the trade-offs more broadly, recognizing that the price society pays for technologically progressive industry may include a concentrated market structure, and inefficient R and D allocation, as well as restricted use of particular new techniques.

However, this view of the capitalist engine is too simple. In particular, it reprises important differences among aspects of, or kinds of, technological knowledge. Also, the institutional richness of real capitalist systems is much greater than depicted in simple models or analyses.

It is important to distinguish among two different aspects of a technology. On the one hand a technology consists of a body of knowledge, which I shall call generic, in the form of a number of generalizations about how things work, key variables influencing performance, the nature of the currently binding constraints and approaches to pushing these back, widely applicable problem solving heuristics, etcetera. I have called this the 'logy' of technology. Giovanni Dosi has used the term 'technological paradigm' to refer to this body of knowledge.[3] Generic knowledge tends to be codified in applied scientific fields like electrical engineering, or materials science, or pharmacology, which are 'about' technologies. On the other hand, a technology also comprises a collection of specific ways of doing things, or artifacts, that are known to be effective in achieving their

---

[2] Nordhaus (1969, ch. 24).
[3] Dosi (1982).

ends if performed with reasonable skill in the appropriate context. These comprise the currently operative 'techniques' of a technology.

Techniques differ significantly in their range of application. Some are potentially valuable to a wide range of users in perhaps a wide range of circumstances. Others are sufficiently narrow in the context of applicability that they have value to only one or a small number of users, being tailored to the idiosyncratic attributes of their products or processes.

If these distinctions are recognized, it becomes clear that different aspects or kinds of technology vary in their latent 'publicness'. The generic aspects of technology have strong latent public good properties, in that restriction of access to that knowledge diminishes the capabilities, perhaps greatly, of those denied access. Widely applicable techniques also may have strong public good properties. Idiosyncratic techniques, on the other hand, have little latent publicness. So the picture of 'technology' as being latently a public good built into simple models fails to make important distinctions.

The view of available instruments, and particularly of institutional structure, built into the standard description also is too simple. There is much more to the capitalist engine than for-profit firms in rivalrous competition. There are, as well, mechanisms through which firms share technological knowledge and cooperate on certain kinds of R and D. There are universities in it, and professional societies. There are public monies that finance large portions of the system as well as private funds.

Once institutional richness is recognized, along with different aspects and kinds of technological knowledge, the simple 'trade-off' view of the matter needs to be supplemented by another one. One can see the task of institutional design as somehow to get the best of both worlds. Establish and preserve property rights, at least to some degree, where profit incentives are effective in stimulating action, and where the costs of keeping knowledge private are not high. Share knowledge where it is efficient to do so, and the cost in terms of diminished incentives is small. Do the work cooperatively, or fund it publicly, and make public those aspects of technology where the advantages of open access are greatest, or where proprietary claims are difficult to police. In my view the capitalist engine is as effective as it is because it has solved this 'institutional assignments' problem not optimally, but reasonably well.[4]

In the remainder of this chapter I shall be concerned with the cooperative and public aspects of technological knowledge, and the institutions supporting public knowledge. In the following chapter I shall consider government R and D support programs.

(B) Technology sharing

Private R and D yields proprietary knowledge, initially. But that knowledge does not stay private; it leaks away and becomes public. Patents seldom hold completely; in most cases they can be invented around. The written patent itself

---

[4] The discussion here is much in the tradition of what has been called the 'new institutional economics'. See, for example, Williamson (1985) and Langlois (1986).

provides some clues as to how to do this. And in any case, the patent lapses after a number of years. The secrecy walls put around some aspect of technology tend to be permeable. Among other things, scientists and engineers move from one company to another, and in so doing bring knowledge of what their former company was doing. A headstart is just that. After a lag, competitors can follow. As I stressed earlier, the fact that initially proprietary knowledge ultimately goes public is both a boon and a problem. This is what the 'trade-off' is all about.

At first thought, one might presume that firms that create new technology ought to exert strong efforts to hold back that technology from going public, and in many instances they clearly do. It is interesting, however, that in some cases firms take positive action to make their proprietary knowledge more public. They engage in patent licensing and in many cases are members of patent pools. In a number of industries patents are not vigorously enforced by their possessors.

Patent licensing would seem easy enough to explain. Firms license other firms because extending the range of use of the invention in that way enhances total profits, and the licensor is able to get a share of the increment. Thus in this way firms are able, through contracting, to cut down on the efficiency losses associated with privatization of a public good.

The presence of patent pools, and industries where it is well known that, as a rule, patents will not be enforced, reflects something different: an apparent agreement among a group of firms that they are all better off if they make a common big pool of at least some of their technological knowledge, than if they all tried to keep their individual pools private. There is a possible problem here, of course, of free riders. Conversations with people in industries where these arrangements exist indicate that patent pools tend to be limited to firms that are active in R and D and hence are contributing to the common pool, and that patent suits are likely to arise when non-contributors to a technology pool are known to be drawing significantly from it. Again, firms have worked out arrangements to mutually exploit the gains of making technological knowledge public.

Eric von Hippel has reported on the practice of 'technology sharing' that is prevalent in several industries he is studying.[5] When a firm faces a technological problem, an engineer in that firm is likely to call up an engineer he knows in another firm, and ask him if he knows about this problem, and if so, whether he knows the solution. In many cases the response is information as to how the problem was solved. Von Hippel notes that when such information is given by one engineer to another, an obligation is established whereby the latter implicitly agrees to provide information to the former when the former asks, and the information is at hand to be given. This type of information swapping apparently tends to be most prevalent when the information involved is not of major proprietary importance to the informing firm, in the sense that it would lose a significant advantage over its rivals by divulging that information. But within the limits set by that constraint, again voluntary com-

---

[5] Von Hippel (1986).

munication is acting to keep down the costs of a proprietary system.

Robert Allen tells an interesting story in which a group of firms enhanced the abilities of each of them to achieve technological advances by keeping open, rather than blocking access to, information about what their individual efforts at advancing technology had achieved.[6] The particular context was marked by the fact that it was easier and less risky to try small increments from current best practice, than to hazard large jumps. This was a context, therefore, where a successful technological advance made by one firm could provide useful information for another firm who might want to hazard going a bit farther in the direction successfully explored by the former, if the former made open information regarding what it had done, and how well it had achieved. In fact, the firms in the industry did divulge that information to their competitors. Thus the efficiency of technical change was enhanced beyond what it would have been had the information been kept strictly proprietary.

In both the case studied by Von Hippel and, I suspect, that studied by Allen, the firms making their technological information public avoided free rider problems by expecting and presumably demanding reciprocity as a condition for continuing with the relationship. So these arrangements appear to be contract-like. Another common element would appear to be this. The firms engaged in the information swapping tended to be a small part of a larger industry. Thus by swapping information they could advantage themselves

[6] Allen (1983).

as a group, relative to other parts of the industry.

It is interesting, however, that many industries have a mechanism for sharing certain types of technological information industry wide. Engineering or technical societies have exactly this function. I have not seen any detailed study which describes the kind of information made public and disseminated through these societies. The regression analysis reported earlier suggests that they provide a mechanism through which upstream firms can communicate new technological developments to their 'market' with the objective of enhancing sales, and users can signal their needs. Eric von Hippel suggests that contact of people at technical societies provides the network through which proceeds the technology sharing he describes.

(C) Cooperative R and D

The foregoing discussion suggests several different arenas where one would not be surprised to see R and D cooperation. I consider several in this section.[7]

One is upstream–downstream R and D cooperation. Earlier I noted the role of upstream firms in technical change in an industry. Often the contribution of upstream firms comes in the form of standardized equipment or materials, but in many cases new equipment needs to be tailored to the particular idiosyncratic needs of the user. In addition, the user may need to modify other aspects of its processes or products in order to take advantage of the potentialities afforded by new materials or equipment.

---

[7] For a more complete canvas, see Haklisch et al. (1984).

Under these circumstances, in-industry and upstream R and D are complements.

Because of this complementarity, and the need to exchange knowledge, cooperative R and D arrangements between a company and an upstream firm, often an equipment supplier, are common. These arrangements may be informal, but often are contractual, as when a firm contracts with an upstream firm to get a particular piece of equipment developed, and also lends its own efforts to that endeavor. In many cases close and durable relationships grow up between a company in a line of business and a particular equipment supplier, involving interchange of information and certain kinds of joint work.

There clearly are some delicate 'appropriability' and 'proprietary' knowledge leakage problems about these upstream – downstream cooperative arrangements. In particular the downstream partner may not be able to control the manner in which the upstream partner deals with the downstream firm's competitors. The conditions in which these vertical arrangements thrive thus are likely to involve either strongly idiosyncratic process needs, or long term pairing, almost a partial merger, of upstream and downstream firms, or acceptance in the downstream firm that the kind of process technology being worked on will not be a competitive item strongly differentiating firms in that industry.

There also are modes of R and D cooperation among firms in the same line of business, although these tend to be more circumscribed. There has long been a tradition of exchange of technological information and cross licensing, between firms in the same line of business, but operating in quite different markets. Cross national inter-firm ties of this sort have been common in many industries. These arrangements reflect mutual agreement that the market is divided, or in the case of cartels, are part of the mechanism to divide the market. When there is such an agreement, mutual help may be a positive sum game. In recent years there has been a surge of joint R and D ventures by companies in different countries in aircraft and electronics. While not necessarily chips off the old block, many are associated with market division.

In the United States, regional public utilities like electric power companies, or regional telephone companies, are in a similar situation. They are not in competition with each other. At the same time they, as a group, can benefit from better technology. It is understandable, therefore, that two of the largest cooperative R and D organizations in the country have been formed to serve these firms; Bellcorp in the case of telephones and EPRI in the case of electric power.

Even where firms are rivalrous, they often exchange some information if the conditions are right, as noted in the previous section. Rivalrous firms also may forge agreement to get done cooperatively certain kinds of research where the results are difficult to keep proprietary, or it would be disadvantageous to the group as a whole to do so. There often are industry-wide problems like learning how better to grade and test raw materials. In many instances an industry can collectively benefit by devising and generally accepting certain uniform practices or standards, particularly for the products of upstream industries. There is a tradition in many industries of trying to fund this type of work collectively, through some kind of an agreed upon voluntary tax formula, and getting it undertaken through trade associations, or at universities or independent laboratories. There are obvious free rider limits on this mechanism, however.

In industries closely linked with science, the results of generic research have strong latent public good properties and are difficult to wall off. Only a few generally very large firms engage in much of this work. Most of it is undertaken at universities, as I shall elaborate shortly.

However, in the past ten years or so, in several industries groups of firms have come together to finance and get done generic research through formal cooperative research arrangements. One important recent example is the Microelectronics and Computer technology Corporation (MCC). The involved companies bought into the arrangement because of a belief that their contributed funds would be highly leveraged, giving them access to a research program, or portions thereof, in which the total resources significantly exceeded their own contribution. The argument also has been put forth that, by pooling funds, a more rational R and D portfolio can be worked out for the group as a whole, and the firms together can gain economies of scale and scope. Put more generally, by treating generic knowledge as public good for the group, and by financing it as such, the involved firms are gaining efficiency advantages.

It should be noted that MCC is not an institution intended to develop proprietary products and processes, but rather to create generic knowledge that member firms can use to create such. It is viewed as a complement to proprietary rivalrous R and D, not a substitute.

The issue, of course, is what the members of the program will get that firms who are not members and who do not contribute funds, will not get. In the case in question, the proposed answer is early access, which is important in industries like semi-conductors and computers, because of the advantage of a headstart and strong learning curve effects. The mechanism that is supposed to assure effective early access is the involvement of company researchers in the MCC projects of greatest interest to them, who are expected to serve a liaison role. MCC is still young, and there is not yet enough experience to test whether the member companies will be able to gain enough advantage over outsiders from this and possibly other technology transfer mechanisms to keep their interest and funding.

Cooperative R and D consortia involving companies that are rivalrous in other respects are presently in style. However, perhaps they should better be regarded as a set of experiments, many of which likely will fail, than as major durable new pieces of the institutional landscape. The free rider problem is a major one. For many years prior to World War II leaders of American industry argued that business should support research at universities, but such support remained modest. Major increases in basic research funding at the universities awaited the mounting of government programs for that purpose. If there is to be durable support for industry oriented generic research programs, significant public monies may be required. And then there is the question of how such programs should be organized and located. As noted above, industry associations never have been particularly important in the R and D game. The traditional home of industry oriented generic research has been the universities.

(D) The role of universities

Universities are an important part of the R and D system. They are a recognized repository of public scientific and technological knowledge. They draw on it in their teaching. They add to it through their research.

Within the United States, university science and engineering, and our science based industries, grew up together. Chemistry took hold as an academic field at about the same time that chemists began to play an important role in industry. The rise of university research, and teaching, in the field of electricity, occurred as the electrical equipment industry began to grow up in the United States. In both cases the universities provided the industry with its technical people, and many of its ideas about product and process innovation.[8]

Contrary to notions that academic science and scientists stand at some distance from industry, save to provide the latter with people, and the basic knowledge needed to create technological breakthroughs, in many fields the links between academic science and industrial science traditionally have been close. Consulting by academic scientists and engineers is not a new phenomenon. And industry scientists long have played a role as advisors to academic science and engineering departments, and as trustees at universities like

---

[8] Noble (1977), Rosenberg (1985).

MIT, who were training people and doing research of relevance to industry.

Of course there have been and are significant differences across scientific fields and across universities. Some fields of academic science, like astronomy, have had only limited contact with industry. Some academic institutions, particularly the members of the old Ivy league, have tended to keep something of a distance from industry. On the other hand, from their beginnings, the land grant universities and the engineering schools have had strong industry ties.

Academic science departments can be important to technical change in industry for two quite different reasons; because of the training they provide young scientists and engineers who go into industry, and because of the research they do. Academics may be able to teach what new industrial scientists need to know, without having their research be particularly relevant to industry. Basic scientific principles and research techniques may be highly important for a young scientist going on in industry to learn, even if the research being done by academics stands at some distance from what is going on in industry. In some technologies, academic research may be illuminating the opportunities and providing the key insights for R and D, but in others the cutting edge of industrial R and D may be far away from academic science.

The situation is dynamic not static. There is evidence that academic research in chemistry and in electrical engineering, has over the years diminished as a source of important new knowledge for industry. Academic researchers were very important to technological developments in the early days of the semi-conductor industry, but as time went by, research and development in industry increasingly separated itself from what the academics were doing. As I will document in a moment, at the current time academic biology and computer science are very important sources of new ideas and techniques for industry. The latter is a new field, and the former is experiencing a renaissance.

Earlier I described how our questionnaire probed at the links of industries with various fields of science. We also asked our respondents to score, on the same scale, the relevance of university research in that field.

The fact that an industry rated a field of science as highly relevant by no means implies that it so rated university research in that field. Thus while 73 industries rated the relevance of chemistry as a field at five or greater, only 19 industries rated university research in chemistry that highly. Forty-four industries rated the relevance of physics at five or greater, but only four gave that high a score to university research in physics. This does not mean that academic research in physics is unimportant over the long run to technical advance in industry. However, the impact likely will be stretched out and indirect, operating through influences on the applied sciences and the engineering disciplines, with the ultimate impact on industrial R and D occurring through these.

What fields of university research have widespread reported relevance to industry, in the sense that a number of industries accredited university research in that field with a relevance score of five or more? Computer science and material science head the list, each with more than 25 industries giving such a score, followed by metallurgy and chemistry, with 21 and 19 industries respectively.

Biology and the applied biological sciences (medical and agricultural science) appear somewhat special today. While these fields are deemed relevant by only a narrow range of industries, those industries that scored these fields at five or higher almost always rated university research in these fields at five or higher too. Thus at the present time those industries whose technologies rest on the basic and applied biological sciences seem to be closely tied to the universities for research as well as training. The same seems true for computer science.

Let me link back to my earlier discussion of generic technological knowledge. Academic research probes new ways of looking at things, develops and tests theories, experiments with new techniques. When academic research in a science is making rapid progress, and when that progress has implications regarding technology, then technical change in that field tends to be driven by change in generic knowledge created in the university system.

Earlier I noted that industries where academic research was important tended to be R and D intensive. For the most part, academic findings or new theories or new techniques do not themselves amount to new technology. Rather they point the way for industrial R and D to be productive. And when academic research is important in this way, a large part of the basis for technological knowledge is, willy-nilly, public knowledge. In contrast, in industries based on technologies whose generic knowledge bases is not being much influenced by academic research, grip on the relevant knowledge for technological change resides largely in industry, and is more proprietary.

Industries where technological advance is being fed significantly by academic research naturally look for close links with university scientists and laboratories where that work is being done. I noted earlier that, traditionally, academia has been quite open to those linkages. However, in recent years there has been an explosion of new arrangements whereby a single firm or a group of firms funds research at a university laboratory, and receives some sort of advantaged access to that research or its findings. Not surprisingly, the industries most engaged in these activities are ones where firms are large, and who rate academic research as highly important to technological change of interest to them. The major such industries are pharmaceuticals and semi-conductors. And the fields of university science being tapped by those arrangements tend to be those where academic research was judged highly relevant to technological advance in those industries, the biological sciences and computer science.[9]

My conjecture is that these kinds of new arrangements for industry support of generic research will prove more durable than the self-standing industry cooperatives. The same free rider problems and technology transfer problems are there, and this limits the magnitude of industry funding. But there are also other parties interested in sustaining the arrangements. The universities themselves, for one. These arrangements are becoming an important part of academic research and teaching in the affected fields. Federal and

[9] For a survey and analysis of recent developments, see Government–University–Industry Research Roundtable (1986).

state governments, for another. Considerable public funding goes into the key academic fields involved, and increasingly an articulated rationale for such public support has been the fostering of technical progress.

Chapter 5

GOVERNMENT SUPPORT OF TECHNICAL ADVANCE IN INDUSTRY[1]

It is apparent that the capitalist engine is a complicated one. The preceding chapter was concerned with describing various features of the variegated institutional landscape. The focus in this chapter is on the roles played by government. Particularly in the post-World War II era, but even before, government programs and finance have been an important part of the system. Below I will describe certain broad classes of government R and D support programs, give some details of particular examples and evaluate the record. But before getting involved in this, I want to set the stage by discussing how the institutional context described in the last two chapters invites, constrains and requires government participation in technical progress.

(A) The context for government action

The Schumpeterian system has been an extraordinarily effective engine of progress. It has shown sensitivity to changing patterns of demand by consumers. The pay off to a firm lies not simply in producing a technologically advanced product, but a product that consumers will buy in quantities at

---

[1] This chapter draws on material in Nelson (1986b).

a price that is profitable. Profitable companies and technologically progressive industries are characterized by strong market research, as well as by strong R and D. At the same time competition among firms, accompanied by secrecy about just where each is laying its technological bets, willy-nilly generates a reasonable diversity of approaches to problems and new products offered to the market for selection.

However, a careful scrutiny either of the models that capture in abstract form the nature of Schumpeterian competition, or of the empirical history of technological advance in any field, indicates that the portfolio generated by market competition can in no way be considered optimum. There is virtually certain to be a clustering of effort verging on duplication, on alternatives widely regarded as promising, and often a neglect of long shots that from society's point of view ought to be explored as a hedge. The premium placed on achieving an invention first, so as to get a patent or at least a headstart, may lead to undue haste and waste and duplication of effort. That three companies – McDonnell–Douglas, Lockheed and the Airbus consortium – all tried to compete in the market for wide-bodied, medium-sized airliners surely meant that total costs were excessive, if it also meant that the airlines got a good deal.

On the other hand, the fact that certain kinds of technological advances are not well protected by patents and are readily copied, deters companies from investing in these, even though a significant advance would lead to enhanced efficiency or performance. Before the advent of hybrid corn seeds, which cannot be reproduced by farmers, seed companies had little incentive to do R and D on new seeds, since the farmers, after buying a batch, simply could reproduce them themselves. The farmers themselves had little incentive to do such work since each was small and had limited opportunities to gain by having a better crop than a neighbor. Within an industry, different kinds of problems vary in the extent to which the problem solver gains a special advantage. In an industry where scientists and engineers are mobile it is hard to keep secret for very long information about the broad operating characteristics of a particular generic design, or about the properties of certain materials. Such knowledge is not patentable and, if patentable, would be very hard to police.

It is tempting to regard these kinds of 'market failures' as providing both justification and guidance for governmental actions to complement, substitute for or guide private initiatives. At the least their recognition guards against the simplistic position that the R and D allocation naturally induced by market forces is in any sense 'optimal'. However, propositions about where and how market forces work poorly cannot alone carry the policy discussion very far.

Market institutions themselves constrain public policies. The fact that much of technological knowledge is proprietary is an important constraint. In the general run of things, a company will not willingly disclose to its competitors or to a public agency, the way it thinks the technological bets ought to be laid. As a result, a government agency may be cut off from the most knowledgeable expertise on the question. While a portion of relevant technological knowledge is public, the details of what works well and what the key problems are, may be known only to the firms in the industry and perhaps their customers. Market knowledge may be very difficult for a government agency to obtain, unless the companies want to give it. Relatedly, a government agency may be sorely limited in its ability to find out where private companies are allocating their own R and D efforts. To the extent that public monies aim to 'fill gaps' in the private R and D portfolio, it may not be easy to identify where these gaps are. There also is a danger that public funds may duplicate, or replace, private funds.

Also, private firms are likely to resist governmental programs that they see as cutting into their own turf, or as likely to aid competitors. It generally is a mistake to think that an industrial policy can successfully be imposed upon an industry. To be effective a policy requires a degree of cooperation and participation from the industry, and members of the industry inevitably are going to be influential in shaping any policy. This is a different thing from saying that the firms in the industry inevitably will control a policy. However, they need to be understood as active players in the game, and not as passive acceptors of government policies and orders.

Institutional complexity.   The central theme of the preceding chapter, of course, was that there was much more to the capitalist engine than for-profit firms in rivalrous competition with each other, and proprietary technologies. There are as well modes of R and D cooperation among firms, and institutions dedicated to public knowledge, like universities and technical societies. In good part these institutions stem from private initiative and deal with what otherwise would be 'market failures'. But these institutions also reflect government policies and are what they are because of these. They also are vehicles through which government policies work. Government policies have a wider range of options because of them.

(B) Types of governmental R and D support programs

I have found it useful to think in terms of three roughly distinguishable kinds of publicly funded R and D programs directed towards enhancing the technological competence of industry: those that mainly support generic research, those that are basically concerned with government procurement, and those that explicitly aim to promote commercial capabilities. These different kinds of programs accommodate, or avoid, or get through, informational and political constraints on government industrial R and D support in different ways, and through different institutions.

Support of scientific and engineering research and education, largely at universities, has long been a recognized government responsibility. Much of this publicly supported activity goes on in the standard academic basic scientific departments, like physics, which do not have tight links with particular technologies or industries. But a good portion of governmentally supported university based research and teaching is in the applied sciences – like pharmacology, metallurgy, computer science, or electrical engineering – which tend to be quite close to certain technologies and industries. Recall that these kinds of sciences were often rated highly relevant by large numbers of industries.

Earlier I stressed that the existence of these applied scientific disciplines partly reflects, and partly assures, that technological knowledge has an important public component as well as a private one. The public part of technological knowledge generally is generic. While such knowledge sometimes can be protected by industrial secrecy, this may be difficult. Also, this is the kind of knowledge that must be imparted to those trained to be engineers or advanced technicians. Therefore, it would seriously interfere with the ability of technical schools and universities, to provide good training if the relevant knowledge were proprietary.

Research in the applied sciences is conducted by scientists and engineers in industry as well as in universities. In some fields, as now seems to be the case in certain areas of semiconductor and computer technology, the industrial R and D groups may be doing more advanced work, at least in certain important dimensions, than the academics. In other cases industry basic research is conducted largely to provide a window into academic research. But in any case, good communication between industrial scientists and academic scientists is an important part of the enterprise. The journals generally receive contributions from both. The scientific societies include both.

The presence of well established networks of applied research scientists, drawn from industry as well as academia, provides one important base for government research support. So long as the R and D support program sticks close to generic work, the problem of proprietary rights is largely averted. A consultative structure already stands to help map out sensible allocations.

Public procurement demands are another traditional source of public involvement in industrial R and D. From far back in history, sovereigns have maintained arsenals and other workshops producing the goods they needed, and concerned themselves with the adequacy of supply of military and other items. While defense is the largest procurement interest, in several countries space agencies, telecommunications networks, electric utilities and airlines are government operated and controlled, and are important sources of demand for high technology products. A strong procurement interest at once yields political legitimacy to a program, and usually is associated with in-house governmental technological expertise. Also, a government agency has some ideas about what kinds of products it wants.

While procurement oriented policies may involve support of generic research to enhance general design capabilities in a particular field, such policies tend to be more narrowly focused than more general generic research support policies, and to be aimed at developing and bringing into production particular products. In contrast with more broadly oriented generic research support programs, where there generally is considerable reliance on the relevant scientific or technical community for guidance, procurement oriented policies tend to be tightly controlled by government agencies pursuing their own ends as they see them.

Policies that stress generic research or procurement, do not directly engage the state in attempting to assure the viability in commercial competition of particular industries, firms or products. But some government R and D support programs are explicitly aimed to promote commercial goals. While support of generic research and technical education may be part of an industry promotion program, such programs tend to focus quite directly on enhancing the commercial competence of national firms. The commitment to a particular industry often is connected to a procurement – generally national security linked – interest, but in the promotional programs the aim is not on particular procurement objectives but to develop or preserve a commercially viable industry. Indeed in some such programs, procurement might be better regarded as an instrument used to further the industry, than vice versa.

Policies expressly aimed at promotion of commercial competence vary in the extent to which the industry itself provides support and guidance for the program, and government in effect facilitates, coordinates and funds, and the extent to which a government agency itself lays out the agenda and the firms largely follow a government lead. Programs which are guided by industry both tap industry expertise and are supported politically by the industry. Such programs also tend to be constrained by the interests of the firms in the industry, as they see them. A program in which the government leads, on the other hand, requires that somehow the government makes judgments about the nature of the market and competition in the industry, as well as about technological matters. But such a program does give the government capability to plan the evolution of technology, for better or worse.

Many government R and D programs of course involve a mix of purposes and activities. An interesting question is, when there is such a mix, do the components complement each other, or clash?

(C) Some case studies

In this section I present three case studies of programs that have had a significant impact on civilian technology. The first one is of U.S. support of R and D in agriculture, a case from which much can be learned. Then I turn to programs in support of semi-conductors and computers, in several countries. I then consider civil aircraft. These three cases are quite different, and their differences warrant pondering.

U.S. agriculture.[2]   Support by the federal and state governments of agricultural research goes back many years. By the mid-19th century, a number of individual states were supporting agricultural experimentation stations, and the federal government was operating one under the auspices of the patent office. The Land Grant College Act of 1864, which established funding for state universities oriented toward the agricultural and mechanical arts, and the Hatch Act of 1887, which provided for federal funding of agricultural research in each state, established the basic legal structure and institutional apparatus for the federal–state

---

[2] There are many good studies of the programs discussed here. I have drawn heavily from Evenson (1982).

cooperation which still exists.

The current system consists both of federal (United States Department of Agriculture) and state units. Most state units are integrated with land grant universities. Many of the researchers hold university teaching positions.

In terms of the kinds of programs discussed earlier, the agricultural program involves a blend of generic and promotional elements. There is no link to any obvious governmental procurement interest, although ironically the federal government has been drawn into supporting the markets for the agricultural products produced by the enormously productive system its R and D support has helped to create. The program, from the beginning, has been called forth by political pressure from farmers, and guided through mechanisms that we shall consider shortly.

Intellectually grounded in such traditional fundamental sciences as chemistry and biology, the system of publicly supported agricultural research has given birth to a large number of applied sciences, such as plant breeding and animal husbandry. Much of the work within these fields is generic, in that research is aimed to enhance understanding relevant to a wide range of problems. They form an intellectual bridge from the fundamental sciences to the practical problems of agriculture that can be attacked by science. Historians of technological advance in agriculture have argued that the applied research and development efforts of the experimentation stations did not yield particularly high rates of return until there was in place a relatively solid scientific understanding of the relevant underlying phenomema. Thus modern hybridization did not go forward effectively until Schull discovered and understood, that to get good hybrids one generally needed to start with pure varieties.

The typology sketched earlier suggests that public support of generic research relevant to agriculture should be looked at somewhat differently than public support of research of direct and immediate relevance to farmers. The agricultural generic research system has much in common with other generic research systems oriented toward particular industries or technologies. Governments have provided support for such generic research systems, across a wide front of industries. However, in such fields as medicine, the publicly supported part of the system (in the United States financed largely through the National Institutes of Health) rarely has ventured beyond generic research. The applied research and development which has a significant chance of leading to proprietary products, has been left largely to private industry.

What is it about farming that has led the 'firms' in this industry to actively demand, not resist, government R and D support of applied work, as well as generic? One factor is that individual farmers, unlike individual firms in many manufacturing industries (like pharmaceuticals), are not in rivalrous competition with each other. It does not hurt one farmer if his neighbor becomes more productive. Put another way, there is very little proprietary knowledge among farmers. At the same time, regional groups of farmers perceive that their sales can be enhanced and their profits increased if their productivity and the quality of their crops are improved. Thus a regional group of farmers has a strong interest in getting effective applied research and development undertaken aimed to enable them, as a group, to become more competitive.

At the present time, state financing of agricultural research is significantly larger than federal financing. The size and character of a state program is effectively molded by the agricultural interests in the state. Experimentation station directors have to justify their budgets in state legislatures, within which farmers carry considerable influence. While the federal part of the system provides some mechanism for coordination, and for supporting work for which no particular state has an especially sharp interest, the system as a whole is very decentralized. Some current critics of the system, speaking from the vantage point of the U.S. Department of Agriculture, or from the basic scientific community, have complained about duplication of effort and lack of coordination. However, the governing structure certainly has made the system responsive and accountable to farming interests as the farmers see them.

Semi-conductors and computers.[3]   U.S. policies in support of semi-conductors and computers have been closely tied to defense objectives and, in particular, to military and space procurement. The United States government had little to do with the work that led to the initial transistor. However, once the transistor had been invented the Department of Defense very quickly understood the potentials of the new

---

[3] Here I draw from the following sources, among others. Levin (1982) and Katz and Phillips (1982), Malerba (1985) and Peck (1983).

technology for military hardware. It financed a considerable amount of research on semi-conductors, but more important as things turned out, induced private companies to invest their own monies in anticipation of major defense contracts. There is no hint that anybody in government had in mind the creation of a new industry that would produce goods for a civilian as well as a government market. However, it turned out that the semi-conductor technologies of use to the military also had widespread civil applications.

Computer technology and semi-conductor technology have been closely intertwined for the last quarter century. In contrast with the semi-conductor case, the U.S. government played a central role in the birth of the modern computer. The government was almost the sole market for the early operational computers, and continued to be the dominant market until the early 1960s. By the mid-1960s, of course, a vast civilian market for computers began to open up. Again, as was the case with transistors and integrated circuits, the strong early government market provided U.S. companies with experience in technology that foreign companies could not match, at least for a long time. But, as was the case with semi-conductors, building a commercially formidable computer industry was a by-product, not a goal, of the government programs.

The Japanese story is, of course, very different. In the first place, throughout the period in question Japanese military research and development and procurement has been on a tight leash, and government programs have had the express purpose of enhancing the commercial capabilities of the Japanese industries. In the second place,

Japanese traditions and ideology regarding the role of
government in guiding the economy are very different than
the American. MITI, and associated contemporary
Japanese government agencies, have grown out of an involvement of the Japanese government in economic plan-
ning and commercial entrepreneurship, that dates back to
the late 19th century.

MITI support of research and development in microelectronics dates back before the VLSI program; however, VLSI
clearly marks a watershed during which the Japanese
government committed itself to sustained support of electronics in Japan. Enough has been written about the VLSI
program so that a detailed discussion here is not warranted.
Suffice it to say that the MITI sponsored part of VLSI was
about what was called 'precompetitive research'. For all
practical purposes, 'precompetitive research' yields what I
earlier called generic technological knowledge. The argument, or the rationale, was put forth that it was highly appropriate and perhaps even necessary for the firms to band
together to do this kind of research cooperatively, and then
go on to do proprietary process and product design
separately and in competition with each other. These ideas
now are part of the general mind set in the United States and
Europe, as well as in Japan.

The European programs in support of semi-conductors
and computers are worthy of brief consideration mainly
because they evidently have not been successful. In France
and Britain, until recently at least, much of the support of
these industries has been tied to military procurement interests. However, the French and British defense programs

have been small compared with the Americans, and have never reached so far technologically. Thus these programs have never pulled French and British firms ahead of where the Americans had been sometime earlier.

Unlike the case in the United States, French policy makers were explicitly interested in enhancing civilian commercial capabilities as well as military ones. Also, in contrast with both the Americans and the Japanese, who aimed to keep a competitive pluralistic home industry, French policies have been marked by an attempt to identify a single 'national champion' in a field, and also, by detailed governmental involvement in the funding of process and product research and development. The results, evidently, have not been happy.

Over the past few years a variety of new programs have sprung up in Europe: national ones like Alvey, and Pan-European ones like Esprit. I lack the space to discuss these here, save to note how they reflect the Japanese influence.

Aircraft.[4]   The story of government policies in support of civil aviation contains a number of elements in common with the electronics story. However, to a far greater extent than in electronics, governments – particularly the British and French – have financed the development and subsidized the production of particular designs aimed explicitly for a civilian market. The Japanese have, up to recently, been in this business to a lesser degree, although they now seem to have plunged into it.

[4] See Mowery and Rosenberg (1968) and Newhouse (1982).

Except for the case of the supersonic transport, the United States has been unique among the governments considered here in not involving itself much in deliberate direct subsidization of civil aircraft development. During the interwar period the government did take a direct interest in the development of the U.S. aircraft industry. While motivated by the objective of having an industry capable of design and production of first-rate military aircraft, the policies aimed quite broadly to support the industry. The National Advisory Committee on Aeronautics was established in 1915 'to investigate the scientific problems involved in flight and give advice to the military air services and other aviation services of the governments'. NACA's work on engine and airframe streamlining played a major role in enabling the design and development of the DC-3. That aircraft, and the planes that evolved from it, dominated the commercial airliner market from the mid-1930s, until the advent of passenger jet aircraft.

The post-World War II story in the United States is that of 'spillover'. The American postwar pre-eminence in the commercial aircraft business rose directly out of military research and development and procurement contracts. The Boeing 707 was designed in parallel with a plane bought by the air force, and had many design elements in common. The American wide-bodied jets show their origins in military cargo planes, and the engines that powered them. However, until the supersonic transport episode, which I shall discuss later, there were no programs of the U.S. government aimed expressly to help in the development of commercial airliners.

The situation in Britain and France has been quite different. The development of commercial aircraft in Britain, in the years after World War II, proceeded according to a detailed government plan. Most of the planned designs were aborted short of a vehicle ready for market test. The few that were fully developed turned out to be dominated by American aircraft.

Perhaps because, unlike the British, they did not come out of World War II with a large aircraft industry and employment, French governmental ventures pushing the design and production of civil aircraft were, in the early post-World War II years, much more modest than the British. However, the French did design and produce the Caravelle which, for a few years, was relatively successful.

The joint British–French venture to produce a supersonic transport aircraft, the Concorde, stands as perhaps the most dramatic example of what can happen when government agencies decide to act as commercial entrepreneurs, and pay little heed to the market. The original $ 450,000,000 estimate for development costs proved low by a factor of ten. Only the captive French and British airlines could be forced to accept delivery of Concorde when it was finally ready for commercial operation in 1976, and both governments have had to subsidize the operation of the plane. Production was terminated in 1979. Only 16 aircraft were produced.

The United States government also was drawn, or jumped, into the subsidy and direction of a supersonic transport project. The U.S. effort, which was begun several years after the European one was launched, was a direct response to it, as well as a desire to exploit expected 'spillover' from the development of the B70 strategic bomber prototype. Significant amounts of public monies were spent on the project. It was cancelled in 1971, far short of producing a viable aircraft.

The airbus case looks like a different story. Apparently European governments, particularly the French, have learned from the supersonic transport disaster. The design of airbus has been guided by careful market research, and while major public monies are involved, the organization of the project has proceeded as if it were a business commercial venture. While through the late 1970s orders for airbus were slim compared with those for the Lockheed and McDonnell–Douglas planes which were direct competitors, beginning in 1979 airbus orders began to pick up dramatically. While it is still too early to tell if the consortium will make a profit, its planes have sold better than any other European designed airliner ever made.

The fierce competition among the airbus consortium, and the American companies producing competitive aircraft, has led to complaints on the part of the Americans that foreign governments were heavily subsidizing their competitor. The issue of governmental subsidy of commercially oriented R and D in high technology industries is sure to be a contentious matter during the rest of this decade, and into the 1990s.

(D) An appraisal of the record

Over the last several years I have spent a considerable amount of time and effort studying the record of past government programs. What does that record show? While the remarks which follow are obviously my own judgments and controversial, I have found that, to a surprising extent, my assessments are shared by others who are knowledgeable about particular programs.

Generic research support.   Government programs directly supporting generic research have in many cases had a clear positive impact. The research support programs of the National Institutes of Health in the United States, have contributed enormously to understanding of conditions of sickness and health, and in many cases have provided strong clues toward new pharmaceuticals, surgical procedures or other treatment regimes. R and D in the pharmaceutical companies, and those designing and producing medical instruments, draws heavily on what has been learned through NIH supported research. The development of computer science as an academic field is another case where government funding of generic research has contributed enormously to the advancement of technological capabilities, in the fields and industries where that impact was intended. Research probing at what makes for plant growth and sickness, and later at the genetics and biochemistry of it, have had a tremendous impact on yields in agriculture.

These three American programs have in common that, while the funds came from government, the research was located largely at universities. They differ in that support of basic research relevant to agriculture has been coupled with governmental support of applied research and development and, similarly, support of computer science has fed into government funding of R and D on computers. In contrast there has been little applied R and D funding by the U.S. government in the field of pharmaceuticals. However, in all three cases the generic research program had an organization and an integrity of its own.

The rash of new government programs in support of generic research have these U.S. programs much less in mind than they do the Japanese programs in support of generic research, particularly in the fields of semi-conductors and computers. The Japanese programs did not make much use of universities, but rather operated through company laboratories, or through special laboratories established for that purpose. The U.S. Department of Defense also supported a significant amount of generic research in electronics in company laboratories, as well as at universities. But a special feature of the Japanese generic support programs, that obviously has caught many people's attention, is that they were conducted 'cooperatively' in a sense that there were formal organizations established to get companies to work together. This idea that support of generic research should be undertaken in a manner which directly involves industry, and puts two or more companies in a cooperative mode, shows clearly in the European programs Alvey and Eureka. In the VHSIC program, the U.S. Department of Defense self-consciously picked up a leaf from the Japanese notebook. No government money is going into MCC, but the U.S. antitrust laws were changed in a way to permit MCC-like organizations, under the belief that the Japanese experience indicated that these were effective.

In my judgment, the record is clear that public support of generic research relevant to an industry can be an effective tool to enhance technical progress in that industry. There are open questions, however, regarding how to design such programs. Some of the U.S. experience suggests it is highly valuable to locate at least parts in a university setting.

Procurement programs.   The principal question about procurement programs, of course, is whether government agencies are getting what they want at reasonable costs and in a timely manner. There is reason to believe that the procurement system of the United States Department of Defense is sorely deficient in this regard. However, here I address not that issue, but rather the following one. Are procurement related programs powerful and useful vehicles for advancing civilian technologies?

The U.S. experience is revealing here. In the case of semiconductors, computers and civil aircraft, U.S. commercial dominance in these fields, which held through the mid-1970s, is unquestionably associated with military procurement programs and associated military R and D programs, during the 1950s and 1960s. However, if one looks at those bits of history carefully, there are several special features. First, in each case, a radically new technology was coming into being, and the military saw its particular demands as being likely furthered by that technology to a much greater extent than did those who were watching civilian markets. Second, in the case of semi-conductors and computers, the Department of Defense funded a considerable amount of generic research. In these fields it turned out that technological advances that were relevant to the military were of the same family that would enhance the performance of civilian products. In the case of aircraft, several of the planes and the engines wanted by the military were, with some modifications, well adapted to civilian use.

By the middle or late 1960s, civilian demands on the performance of semi-conductors and computers were, in important ways, different than military demands, and in many instances were exerting stronger pulls on the technology than were defense demands. The direction of spillover began to change, with the military increasingly taking advantage of new technologies developed initially with civilian markets as the target. In aircraft, there was a parting of the ways of the desired paths of fighters and bombers on the one hand, and passenger jets on the other. A strong case can be made that by the middle 1970s spillover from DOD supported programs to civil technologies was quite limited.

In my judgment, given the current context, it is foolish to tie one's hopes or fears, regarding commercial competence in an industry, to spillover from military programs. There are many reasons why such spillover is likely to be limited, and to come at very high cost. And there surely are better ways to skin the cat.

Promotion programs.   These are a mixed bag with some good and some bad apples. The long standing American programs in support of applied research and development relating to agriculture have been an important part of the reason for the enormously enhanced productivity, and the strong competitive advantage, of American agriculture. On the other hand, virtually everyone recognizes that the supersonic transport program was a disaster (although there now seem to be some who want to repeat it), and similarly in most countries nuclear power programs have not come close to yielding returns equivalent to the costs.

There is an important difference between the U.S. agricultural R and D support program and the SST and nuclear power cases, which may provide some clues as to necessary (but probably not sufficient) conditions for a government promotional program to avoid being a disaster. The U.S. agricultural programs have been closely under the control of the group which was supposed to benefit from the new technology – the farmers. In contrast, in the SST cases and in the cases of nuclear power, most of the decisions were made from the top, by bureaucrats in government agencies with very little attention being paid to user needs, and constraints.

The case of airbus tends to support this conjecture. While knowledgeable people may disagree as to whether the airbus program ever will yield returns commensurate with the costs, it certainly is nothing like the disaster that the SST was. And it is building aircraft that the airlines are attracted to buy, if the price is right. An important reason for this is that, from the beginning of the operation, a considerable amount of attention has been spent on marketing, on assessing what the airlines wanted to buy, on what the competition was doing, etcetera.

Assume that governments have learned how to undertake promotional projects. They still are quite problematic, in my view, except under very special conditions. This is surely so if they involve massive government subsidy, easily identifiable and right up front. GATT may have a great deal of difficulty in agreeing to rules on this matter which cannot be evaded, but that only signals that these kinds of programs are the stuff of international conflict. That is what is going on right now in the field of large civil aircraft.

Chapter 6

REPRISE

The basic theme of this essay is understanding technical change as an evolutionary process. Let me return to it and its central implications.

Economists, from Smith to Marx to Schumpeter, have touted capitalism as an engine of progress. And surely the technical progress that has been generated over the past two centuries is historically unprecedented. We do not have much to compare it with in its own times, but the industrial R and D systems that have grown up patterned on the Soviet model look strikingly ineffective in comparison.

Perhaps the two striking contrasts with Soviet style systems are the harnessing of profit incentives to innovation, and the existence of multiple, often rivalrous, sources of innovation. The advantages of the former are clear enough. Firms can make money if they innovate to meet a real demand, and can keep some proprietary grip on their innovation. This has led to an innovation system that is attentive to needs and to technological opportunities, and to changes in both of these, to the extent that a firm can appropriate a sufficient share of the returns. Also, a large share of R and D is located in the firms themselves, close to the relevant knowledge. The advantages of giving firms incentives, and hands-on capability, for innovation can be seen most sharply by considering the poor innovation performance of socialist countries where neither of these conditions exists.

But what does the pluralism and rivalry built into the system buy us? Clearly, some troubles. It is the presence of competitors that makes it important to a company to somehow keep others away from the innovations it has created at high cost. But the presence of proprietary restrictions distorts resource allocation in both production and in R and D. And easy diffusion discourages R and D.

Why pay the price of pluralism? Conventional economic theory provides one answer: competition in production is needed to force low price–cost margins, and to approximate Pareto efficiency in allocation among different lines of production. Of course the latter part of the argument is attenuated somewhat if one recognizes that, if R and D is done pluralistically and technology is proprietary, other kinds of inefficiencies are built into the system.

Another answer, less tied to neo-classical notions about efficiency and competition, is this. I would argue that the most important advantage lent the capitalist engine by its built-in pluralism and rivalry is mechanism to cope with the uncertainties innately involved in R and D, and to take advantage of, not repress, differences of opinion.

From the start of this essay I have stressed the essential uncertainties which surround the question: where should R and D resources be allocated in an industry where technology is advancing rapidly? There generally are a wide variety of ways in which the existing technology can be improved, and at least several different paths toward achieving any of these. It is uncertain which of the objectives is most worthwhile pursuing, and which of the approaches will prove most successful.

If the problem were simply uncertainty, but everybody agreed on the structure of the uncertainty, one could define the R and D allocation problem as being something like a huge dynamic programming problem involving uncertainty and learning. An optimum strategy in such a context may well involve exploring a variety of different possibilities, and holding off commitment to a single one until lots of evidence is acquired. There is considerable merit to this perception.

But a key characteristic of the R and D environment is differences of opinion and vision. Human beings and organizations, seem to be innately limited in the range of things they can hold in mind at any time, and even in the way they look at problems. Some individuals simply see things about a problem, or about a possible solution, that others don't see; what is seen may or may not be actually there. The fact that different people look at a problem in different ways and see different things about it means that terms like insight, creativity, genius, often apply to successful inventors or laboratories. And at any time there is inevitable disagreement about what is the best course to take, and about who will be right about the matter this time, even if one could get open unguarded discussion of the question. Committees of experts are unreliable judges of these issues even if, or particularly if, they are forced to arrive at agreement.

What the capitalist engine provides is multiple sources of initiative, and a competition among those who place their bets on different ideas. And it does so in a context where those that lay their bets have every incentive to attend to the market, and there is widespread access to the basic generic technological knowledge one needs to command in order to scan the possible solutions. The capitalist engine lets the market decide, ex post, what were the good ideas and what were the poor ones. This is painful for some, and costly, but given the nature of technological uncertainties, and the way humans and organizations seem to think and behave, perhaps this is the best we can do.

But another part of the system keeps proprietary constraints bounded. Competitors are able to invent around patents. They learn with a lag what innovators have learned. Where large latent public good efficiency possibilities are repressed if the R and D is done within industry, incentives are generated for outsiders to do the R and D. There also is a certain amount of technology sharing or trading. There are modes of R and D cooperation for certain kinds of work.

And universities are an important part of the system. In the U.S., university research has in many areas been closely linked to technology and concern for applications, and not cloistered and separated from them as some academics have argued it ought to be. Public funds have been allocated across fields of university science in a way responsive to perceived practical problems and opportunities. What the university system creates is public, not private. In a number of areas of technology, it is university research that is providing the cutting edge. In other fields that is not the case; however, in most of these the open knowledge available at the university is such that public knowledge is not drastically behind proprietary knowledge.

This open, publicly supported, part of the capitalist engine has solved the problem that, in general, generic knowledge is difficult to keep bottled up and, therefore, there is only limited incentive for profit-oriented firms to invest in its generation. But more than that, this part of the system has staked out areas of knowledge that are kept public. Keeping the important generic knowledge open cuts down on the average triangle loss associated with private innovation, by making it easier for competitors to respond effectively to someone else's innovation. The fact that important generic knowledge is public, not private, means that today's R and D effort can build on the most generally useful part of yesterday's findings. And because the basic knowledge needed to operate a technology is kept open, not private, the chances that a single firm will be able through its own R and D to monopolize the industry in question are kept under control.

It is a complex system for sure, and a messy one. It surely can be improved upon somehow, but no one knows for sure just how to do that; what departures will make it work better, and what changes will make it work worse.

But the capitalist engine also has the advantage that, in the nature of its dynamics, there is continuing experimentation with its own organization, and here, too, there are multiple independent sources of initiative. The modern corporate R and D laboratory itself, the heart of the system, grew up during the early 20th century as a result of bets made by a few scientists and businessmen. Events proved them right and the lesson was learned by other firms. The nature and source of funding, of university research in the United States also has followed an evolutionary pattern, with different kinds of universities doing different things and being open to different kinds of initiatives on the part of business and government. On the other hand, there were many different independent actors in that game in both business and government. As noted earlier, the system of government funding of university research arose only after various other proposals for funding had been tried, and failed.

At the present time there are a lot of organizational experiments going on. Industry cooperation in the finance of generic research is now the rage. In the United States there has been a recent surge of new arrangements linking industry to university research, in some cases initiated by industry, and in some cases initiated through government programs. It is too early to judge whether these will turn out to be successful or not. But they are going on. Such institutional experimentation may be the most durable strength of the system.

BIBLIOGRAPHY

Allen, R.C., 1983, Collective invention, Journal of Economic Behavior and Organization 4, no. 1, 1–24.

Dosi, G., 1982, Technological paradigms and technological trajectories: A suggested interpretation of the determinants and directions of technical change, Research Policy 11, no. 3, 147–162.

Evenson, R., 1982, Technical changes in U.S. agriculture, in: R.R. Nelson, ed., Government and technical progress: A cross industry analysis (Pergamon, Oxford).

Government–University–Industry Research Roundtable, 1986, New alliances and partnerships in American science and engineering (National Academy Press, Washington, DC).

Griliches, Z., 1958, Research costs and social returns: Hybrid corn and related innovations, Journal of Political Economy 76, no. 5, Oct., 419–432.

Haklisch, C., H. Fusfeld and A. Levinson, 1984, Trends in collective industrial research (Center for Science and Technology Policy, New York).

Kalos, S., 1983, The economic impacts of government research and development: The semi conductor experience, Ph.D. dissertation (Yale University, New Haven, CT).

Kamien, M. and N. Schwartz, 1982, Market structure and innovation (Cambridge University Press, Cambridge).

Katz, B. and A. Phillips, 1982, The computer industry, in: R.R. Nelson, ed., Government and technical progress: A cross industry analysis (Pergamon, Oxford).

Kendrick, J., 1961, Productivity trends in the United States (Princeton University Press for the NBER, Princeton, NJ).

Langlois, R.W., ed., 1986, Economics as a process: Essays in the new institutional economics (Cambridge University Press, Cambridge).

Leontief, W., 1966, Domestic production and foreign trade: The American capital position re-examined, in: W. Leontief, ed., Input–output economics (Oxford University Press, Oxford).

Levin, R., 1982, The semi conductor industry, in: R.R. Nelson, ed., Government and technical progress: A cross industry analysis (Pergamon, Oxford).

Levin, R., A. Klevorich, R. Nelson and S. Winter, 1984, Survey research on R and D appropriability and technological opportunity, Part 1: Appropriability, Mimeo. (Yale University, New Haven, CT).

Malerba, F., 1985, The semi conductor business (University of Wisconsin Press, Madison, WI).

Mansfield, E., M. Schwartz and S. Wagner, 1981, Imitation costs and patents: An empirical study, Economic Journal 91, no. 364, Dec., 907–918.

Miller, R. and D. Sawyer, 1968, The technical development of modern aircraft (Routledge and Kegan Paul, London).

Mowery, D. and N. Rosenberg, 1982, Commercial aircraft, in: R.R. Nelson, ed., Government and technical progress: A cross industry analysis (Pergamon, Oxford).

Nelson, R.R., 1981, Research on productivity growth and productivity differences, Journal of Economic Literature 19, no. 3, Sept., 1029–1064.

Nelson, R., 1986a, Evolutionary modelling of economic change, in: J. Stiglitz and G.F. Mathewson, eds., New developments in the analysis of market structure (MIT Press, Cambridge, MA).

Nelson, R., 1986b, The state and private enterprise in high technology industries, in: R.M. MacLeod, ed., Technology and the human prospect: Essays in honor of Christopher Freeman (Pinter, London).

Nelson, R. and S. Winter, 1974, Neoclassical vs. evolutionary theories of economic growth, Economic Journal 84, no. 336, 886–905.

Nelson, R. and S. Winter, 1975, Factor price changes and factor substitution in an evolutionary model, Bell Journal of Economics 6, no. 2, 466–486.

Nelson, R. and S. Winter, 1977, Dynamic competition and technical progress, in: B. Balassa and R. Nelson, eds., Economic progress, private values and public policies: Essays in honour of William Fellner (North-Holland, Amsterdam).

Nelson, R. and S. Winter, 1980, Forces generating and limiting concentration under Schumpeterian competition, Bell Journal of Economics 11, no. 1, 524–548.

Nelson, R. and S. Winter, 1982a, An evolutionary theory of economic change (Harvard University Press, Cambridge, MA).

Nelson, R. and S. Winter, 1982b, The Schumpeterian trade offs revisited, American Economic Review 72, no. 1, March, 114–132.

Newhouse, J., 1982, The sporty game (Knopf, New York).

Noble, D., 1977, America by design (Knopf, New York).

Nordhaus, W.D., 1969, Invention, growth and welfare: A theoretical treatment of technological change (MIT Press, Cambridge, MA).

Peck, M.J., 1983, Government coordination of R and D in the Japanese electronics industry, Mimeo.

Rosenberg, N., 1985, The commercial exploitation of science by American industry, in: K. Clark, R. Hayes and C. Lorenz, eds., The uneasy alliance: Managing the productivity–technology dilemma (Harvard Business School, Cambridge, MA).

Scherer, F.M., 1959, Patents and the corporation, 2nd ed., privately printed.

Taylor, C.T. and Z.A. Silberston, 1973, The economic impact of the patent system: A study of the British experience (Cambridge University Press, Cambridge).

Terleckyj, N., 1980, Direct and indirect effects of industrial research and development on productivity growth of industries, in: J. Kendrick and B. Vaccara, eds., New developments in productivity measurement and analysis (University of Chicago Press for the NBER, Chicago, IL).

Von Hippel, E., 1986, Cooperation between competing firms: Informal know-how trading, Sloan School of Management working paper (MIT, Cambridge, MA).

Williamson, O.E., 1985, The economic institutions of capitalism (The Free Press, New York).